On Love and Loneliness

J. KRISHNAMURTI

KRISHNAMURTI FOUNDATION INDIA

Sources and acknowledgements can be found on page 154

Series editor : Mary Cadogan
Associate editors : Ray McCoy and David Skitt

© 1993 Krishnamurti Foundation Trust Ltd.
Brockwood Park, Bramdean
Hampshire SO24 0LQ, England
E-mail: info@brockwood.org.uk
&
Krishnamurti Foundation of America
P O Box 1560, Ojai, California 93024-1560.
E-mail: kfa@kfa.org

Published, with permission, by
Krishnamurti Foundation India
Vasanta Vihar, 124,126 Greenways Road
Chennai - 600 028.
E-mail: publications@kfionline.org
Website: www.kfionline.org

First Indian edition 2000
Reprinted 2002, 2004, 2006, 2009

Philosophy / Religion
ISBN 81-87326-20-4

Cover photo : F. Grohe
Cover design : Deepa Kamath

Printed by
The Indcom Press
393 Velachery Main Road
Vijaya Nagar, Velachery
Chennai - 600 042.

If you have no love—do what you will, go after all the gods on earth, do all the social activities, try to reform the poor, enter politics, write books, write poems—you are a dead human being. Without love your problems will increase, multiply endlessly. And with love, do what you will, there is no risk, there is no conflict. Then love is the essence of virtue.

Bombay, 21 February 1965

Contents

	Foreword
1	Madras, 16 December 1972
8	Brockwood Park, 11 September 1971
16	With Students at Rajghat School, 19 December 1952
22	Bombay, 12 February 1950
27	Ojai, 28 August 1949
30	Bombay, 12 March 1950
38	New York, 18 June 1950
46	Seattle, 6 August 1950
49	Madras, 3 February 1952
54	Loneliness: From *Commentaries on Living First Series*
58	Discussion with Professor Maurice Wilkins, Brockwood Park, 12 February 1982
67	New York, 24 April 1971: From *The Awakening of Intelligence*
74	Brockwood Park, 30 August 1977
83	Saanen, 18 July 1978
92	Bombay, 31 January 1982
98	With Young People in India: From *Life Ahead*
104	Saanen, 18 July 1968: From *Talks and Dialogues in Saanen 1968*

111	Saanen, 5 August 1962
117	Bombay, 21 February 1965
125	London, 7 April 1953
131	Saanen, 26 July 1973
139	Saanen, 23 July 1974
149	Madras, 5 February 1950
154	Sources and Acknowledgments

Foreword

JIDDU KRISHNAMURTI WAS born in India in 1895 and, at the age of thirteen, was taken up by the Theosophical Society, which considered him to be the vehicle for the "world teacher" whose advent it had been proclaiming. Krishnamurti was soon to emerge as a powerful, uncompromising, and unclassifiable teacher, whose talks and writings were not linked to any specific religion and were of neither the East nor the West but for the whole world. Firmly repudiating the messianic image, in 1929 he dramatically dissolved the large and monied organization that had been built around him and declared truth to be "a pathless land," which could not be approached by any formalized religion, philosophy, or sect.

For the rest of his life Krishnamurti insistently rejected the guru status that others tried to foist upon him. He continued to attract large audiences throughout the world but claimed no authority, wanted no disciples, and spoke always as one individual to another. At the core of his teaching was the realization that fundamental changes in society can be brought about only by a transformation of individual consciousness. The need for self-knowledge and understanding of the restrictive, separative influences of religious and nationalistic conditionings was constantly stressed. Krishnamurti pointed always to the urgent need for openness, for that "vast space in the brain in which there is unimaginable energy."

This seems to have been the wellspring of his own creativity and the key to his catalytic impact on such a wide variety of people.

Krishnamurti continued to speak all over the world until he died in 1986 at the age of ninety. His talks and dialogues, journals and letters, have been preserved in over sixty books and hundreds of recordings. From that vast body of teachings this series of theme books has been compiled. Each book focuses on an issue that has particular relevance to and urgency in our daily lives.

Madras, 16 December 1972

IN TALKING OVER together these questions, which are our daily problems of life, I think we have to bear in mind that we are investigating together; together we are taking a journey into rather complex issues of life, and to investigate together there must be a quality of intensity, a quality of mind that is not tethered to any particular belief or conclusion, but is willing to go very far, not in distance of time, but in depth.

❖

WE ARE GOING to inquire together about whether we can bring about order in our daily life of relationship. Because relationship is society. The relationship between you and me, between me and another, is the structure of society. That is, relationship is the structure and the nature of society. I am putting it very, very simply. And when there is no order in that relationship, as there is at present no order, then every kind of action must be not only contradictory, but must also produce a great deal of sorrow, mischief, confusion, and conflict. Please, don't just let me talk, but share it together, because we are taking a journey together, perhaps hand in hand, with affection, with consideration. If you merely sit down and are talked at, or lectured to, then I am afraid you and I cannot take the journey together hand in hand. So please do observe your own mind, your own relationship—it doesn't matter with whom it is, your wife, your children, with your neighbour, or with your government—and see if there is order in that relationship; because order is necessary, precision is necessary. Order is virtue, order is so mathematical, so pure, complete, and we are going to find out if there is such order.

No one can live without relationship. You may withdraw into the mountains, become a monk, a *sannyasi*, wander off into the desert by yourself, but you are related. You cannot escape from that absolute fact. You cannot exist in isolation. Your mind may think it exists in isolation, or bring about a state of isolation, but even in that isolation you are related. Life is relationship, living is relationship. We cannot live if you and I have built a wall around ourselves and just peep over that wall occasionally. Unconsciously, deeply, under the wall, we are related. I do not think we have paid a great deal of attention to this question of relationship. Your books don't talk about relationship; they talk about God, practice methods, how to breathe, about not doing this or that, but I have been told that relationship is never mentioned.

Relationship implies responsibility, as freedom does. To be related is to live; that is life; that is existence. And if there is disorder in that relationship, our whole society, culture goes to pieces, which is what is happening now.

So what is order, what is freedom, and what is relationship? What is disorder? Because when the mind really deeply, inwardly understands what brings about disorder, then out of that insight, out of that awareness, out of that observation, order naturally comes. It is not a blueprint of what order should be; that is what we have been brought up with—a pattern that has been laid down by religions, by cultures, as to what order should be, or what order is. The mind has tried to conform to that order, whether it is cultural order, social order, legalistic order, or religious order; it has tried to conform to the pattern established by social activity, by certain leaders, teachers. To me that is not order because in that is implied conformity, and where there is conformity, there is disorder. Where there is the acceptance of authority, there is disorder. Where there is comparative existence—that is, measuring yourself against somebody, comparing yourself with somebody—there is disorder. I will show you why.

Why does your mind conform? Have you ever asked? Are you aware that you are conforming to a pattern? It doesn't matter what that pattern is, whether you have established a pattern for yourself or it has been established for you. Why are we always conforming? Where there is conformity there cannot be freedom, obviously. Yet the mind is always seeking freedom—the more intelligent, the more alert, the more aware it is, the greater the demand. The mind conforms, imitates, because there is more security in conformity, in following a pattern. That's an obvious fact. You do all kinds of things socially because it is better to conform. You may be educated abroad, you may be a great scientist, politician, but you always have a sneaking fear that if you don't go to temples or do the ordinary things that you have been told to do, something evil might happen, so you conform. What happens to the mind that conforms? Investigate it, please. What happens to your mind when you conform? First of all, there is a total denial of freedom, total denial of perception, total denial of independent inquiry. When you conform there is fear. Right? From childhood the mind has been trained to imitate, conform to the pattern which society has established—pass examinations, get a degree, if you are lucky get a job, and get married, finished. You accept that pattern, and you are frightened not to follow that pattern.

So inwardly you deny freedom, inwardly you are frightened, inwardly you have a sense of not being free to find out, inquire, search, ask. So that produces disorder in our relationship. You and I are trying to go into this really deeply, to have real insight, see the truth of it; and it is the perception of the truth that frees the mind, not some practice, or the activity of inquiry, but the actual perception of 'what is'.

We bring about disorder in relationship, both inwardly and outwardly, through fear, through conformity, through measurement, which is comparison. Our relationship is in disorder, not only with each other, however intimate it may be, but also outwardly. If we see that disorder clearly, not out there but in here, deeply in ourselves, see all the implications of it, then out of that perception comes order. Then we don't have to live according to an imposed order. Order has no pattern, is not a blueprint; it comes out of the comprehension of what disorder is. The more you understand disorder in relationship, the greater the order. So we have to find out what is our relationship with each other.

What is your relationship with another? Have you any relationship at all; or is your relationship with the past? The past, with its images, experience, knowledge, brings about what you call relationship. But knowledge in relationship causes disorder. I am related to you. I am your son, your father, your wife, your husband. We have lived together; you have hurt me and I have hurt you. You have nagged me, you have bullied me, you have beaten me, you have said hard things behind my back and to my face. So I have lived with you for ten years or two days, and these memories remain, the hurts, the irritations, the sexual pleasures, the annoyances, the brutal words, and so on. Those are recorded in the brain cells which hold memory. So my relationship with you is based on the past. The past is my life. If you have observed, you will see how the mind, your life, your activity, is rooted in the past. Relationship rooted in the past must create disorder. That is, knowledge in relationship brings disorder. If you have hurt me, I remember that; you hurt me yesterday, or a week ago, that remains in my mind, that's the knowledge I have about you. That knowledge prevents relationship; that knowledge in relationship breeds disorder. So the question is: When you hurt me, flatter me, when you scandalize me, can the mind wipe it away at the very moment without recording it? Have you ever tried this?

How lovely that moon is, isn't it, looking through the leaves, and the cry of those crows, and the evening light! That extraordinary moon through the leaves is a wondrous thing. Look at it, enjoy it.[1]

Say, yesterday somebody said rather harsh things to me, which are not true. What he said is recorded, and the mind identifies the person with that record and acts according to that record. Where the mind is acting in relationship with the knowledge of that insult, the harsh words, that untrue thing, then that knowledge in relationship brings disorder. Right? Now, how is the mind not to record at the moment of insult, or at the moment of flattery? Because to me the most important thing in life is relationship. Without relationship there must be disorder. A mind that lives in order, total order, which is the highest form of mathematical order, cannot for a single minute allow the shadow of disorder to come upon it. And that disorder comes into being when the mind acts on the basis of past knowledge in relationship. So how is the mind not to record the insult, but know the insult has been given, as well as flattery? Can it know it has been given, but yet not record it, so the mind is always clean, healthy, whole in relationship?

Are you interested in this? You know, if you are really interested in it, it is the greatest problem in life: how to live a life in relationship, in which the mind has never been hurt, never been distorted. Now, is this possible? We have put an impossible question. It is an impossible question, and we must find the impossible answer. Because what is possible is mediocre, is already finished, done; but if you ask the impossible question, the mind has to find the answer. Can the mind do that? This is love. The mind that records no insult, no flattery, knows what love is.

Can the mind never record, never, absolutely never record the insult or the flattery? Is that possible? If the mind can find the answer to that, one has solved the problem of relationship. We live in relationship. Relationship is not an abstraction, it is a daily, everyday fact. Whether you go to the office, come back and sleep with your wife, or quarrel, you are always in relationship. And if there is no order in that relationship between you and another, or between you and many or one, you will create a culture that will ultimately produce disorder, as is being done now. So order is absolutely essential. To find that out, can the mind, though it has been insulted, hurt, knocked about, had brutal things said to it, never for a second hold it? The moment you hold it, it is already recorded, it has left a mark in the brain cells. See the difficulty of this question. Can the mind do this so that the mind remains totally innocent? A mind that is innocent means a mind that is incapable of being hurt. Because it is incapable of being hurt, it will not hurt another. Now, is this possible? Every form of influence, every form of incident, every form of mischief, distrust, is thrown upon the mind. Can the mind never record and therefore remain very innocent, very clear? We are going to find out together.

We will come to it by asking what love is. Is love the product of thought? Is love in the field of time? Is love pleasure? Is love something that can be cultivated, practised, put together by thought? In inquiring into this, one has to go into the question: Is love pleasure—sexual or any other kind of pleasure? Our mind is pursuing pleasure all the time: yesterday I had a good meal, the pleasure of that meal is recorded and I want more, a better meal or the same kind of meal tomorrow. I have taken great delight in the sunset, or looking at the moon through the leaves, or seeing a wave far out at sea. That beauty gives great delight, and that is great pleasure. The mind records it and wants it repeated. Thought thinks about sex, thinks, chews over it, wants it repeated; and that you call love. Right? Don't be shy when we talk about sex, that's part of your life. You have made it hideous because you have denied every kind of freedom except that one freedom.

So is love pleasure? Is love put together by thought, as pleasure is put together by thought? Is love envy? Can anyone love who is envious, who is greedy, ambitious, violent, conforming, obeying, totally in disorder? So what is love? It is not any of these things, obviously. It is not pleasure. Please understand the importance of pleasure. Pleasure is sustained by thought; therefore thought is not love. Thought cannot cultivate love. It can and does cultivate the pursuit of pleasure, as it does fear, but thought cannot create love, or put it together. See the truth. See it and you will put away your ambition, your greed, altogether. So through negation you come to the most extraordinary thing called love, which is the most positive.

Disorder in relationship means there is no love, and that disorder exists when there is conformity. So a mind that conforms to a pattern of pleasure, or what it thinks is love, can never know what love is. A mind that has understood the whole ripening of disorder comes to an order which is virtue, therefore which is love. It's your life, it's not my life. If you don't live this way, you will be most unhappy, caught in social disorder, and be dragged forever in that stream. It is only the man who steps out of that stream who knows what love is, what order is.

1. *Editor's Note:* The public talks in Madras were held out of doors, in the evening, when it was cooler.

Brockwood Park,
11 September 1971

To FIND OUT anything humanly, mustn't we begin with a certain quality of freedom? If we are to investigate such a complex problem as love, we must come to that investigation with a freedom from all our particular prejudices, idiosyncrasies, and tendencies, our wishes of what love should be—either Victorian or modern. We should put all that aside, if we can, in order to investigate; otherwise we'll be distracted, we'll waste our energy in affirming or contradicting according to our particular conditioning. In talking over this question of what love is, can we see the importance of finding out the full significance and the meaning and the depth of what that word conveys or doesn't convey? Shouldn't we first see if we can free the mind from the various conclusions that it has about that word? Is it possible to liberate the mind, to free the mind, from the deep-rooted prejudices, biases, conclusions? Because to talk over together this question of what love is, it seems to me that we have to have a mind that is very perceptive; and one cannot have such a good, clear mind if one has opinions, judgments, saying this is what love should be or should not be. To examine the mind, our whole inquiry must begin with the sense of freedom—not freedom *from* something, but the quality of freedom that is capable of looking, observing, seeing what truth is. You can go back to your prejudices, your particular vanities and conclusions later, but could we put aside all that for the moment and sustain this freedom in inquiry?

There are several things involved: sex, jealousy, loneliness, the sense of attachment, companionship, a great deal of pleasure, and thereby also fear. Isn't all that involved in that one word? Could we begin with this question of pleasure, because that plays an important part in love? Most religions have denied sex because they say a man who is caught in sensory pleasures cannot possibly understand what truth is, what God is, what love is, what the supreme, immeasurable thing is. This is a prevalent religious conditioning in Christianity, in India, and also in Buddhism. When we are going to look into the question of what love is, we have to be aware of our traditional, inherited conditioning which brings about various forms of suppression—Victorian and modern—or permissive enjoyment of sex.

Pleasure plays an extraordinary part in our life. If you have talked to any of the so-called highly disciplined, intellectual, religious people—I wouldn't call them religious, but they are called religious—you know that chastity is one of their immense problems. You may think all this is totally irrelevant, that chastity has no place in the modern world, and brush it aside. I think that would be a pity because knowing what chastity is, is one of the problems. To go into this question of what love is, one has to have a wide, deep mind to find out, not just make verbal assertions. Why does pleasure play such an important part in our lives? I'm not saying it is right or wrong, we are inquiring; there is no assertion that there should or should not be sex or pleasure. Why does pleasure play such an immense role in every activity of our life? It is one of our primary urges, but why has it assumed such fantastic magnitude, not only in the Western world, where it is so blatant, so vulgar, but also in the East? It is one of our major problems. Why? Religions—so-called religions—the priests, have decried it. If you would seek God, they say, you must take a vow of celibacy. I know a monk in India, a very, very serious man, scholarly, intellectual. At the age of fifteen or sixteen, he gave up the world and took a vow of celibacy. As he grew older—I met him when he was about forty—he gave up those vows and married. He had a hell of a time because Indian culture says it is appalling for a man who has taken a vow to go back. He was ostracized; he went through a very bad time. And that is most people's mentality. Why has sex assumed such fantastic importance?

There is the whole problem of pornography, allowing complete freedom to read, to print, show anything you like, to give freedom from suppression. You know all that goes on in the world. What has love to do with that? What does all this mean—love, sex, pleasure, and chastity? Please don't forget that word or the meaning of that word to which man has given such great importance—to lead a life of chastity. Let's find out why man throughout the ages has given sex such a prominent place in life, and why there is such resistance against it. I don't know how we are going to answer it.

Is not one of the factors that in sexual activity there is total freedom? Intellectually we are imitative, intellectually we are not creative, intellectually we are second-hand, or third-hand; we repeat—repeat what others have said, our little thoughts. There we are not active, creative, alive, free; and emotionally we have no passion, we have no deep interests. We may be enthusiastic, but that soon fades; there isn't a sustained passion, and our life is more or less mechanical, a daily routine. Since it is a life of repetitive reactions which are mechanical, intellectually, technologically, and more or less emotionally, this one other activity naturally becomes extraordinarily important. If there were freedom intellectually and one had deep passion, fire, then sex would have its own place and become quite unimportant. We would not give such tremendous meaning to it, trying to find nirvana through sex, or thinking that through sex we are going to have complete unity with mankind. You know all the things that we hope to find through that!

So can our minds find freedom? Can our minds be tremendously alive and clear, perceptive?—not the perception that we have gathered from others, from the philosophers, psychologists, and the so-called spiritual teachers, who are not spiritual at all. When there is a quality of deep, passionate freedom, then sex has its own place. Then what is chastity? Has chastity any place in our life at all? What is the meaning of that word *chaste*, not the dictionary meaning only, but the deep meaning of it? What does it mean to have a mind that is completely chaste? I think we ought to inquire into that. Perhaps that is much more important.

If one is aware of the whole activity of the mind—without a division as the observer watching the mind and therefore bringing about a conflict between the observer and the observed—doesn't one see the constant shaping of images, and remembrances of various pleasures, misfortunes, accidents, insults, and all the various impressions, influences, and pressures? These crowd our minds. Thought thinks about a sexual act, pictures it, imagines it, sustains evocative emotions, gets excited. Such a mind is not a chaste mind. It is a mind that has no picture at all, no image, that is a chaste mind. Then the mind is always innocent. The word *innocency* means a mind that does not receive hurts—or give hurt; it is incapable of hurting and also incapable of being hurt, but yet is totally vulnerable. Such a mind is a chaste mind. But those people who have taken vows of chastity are not chaste at all; they are battling with themselves everlastingly. I know various monks in the West and in the East, and what tortures they have gone through, all to find God. Their minds are twisted, tortured.

All this is involved in pleasure. Where is pleasure in relation to love? What is the relationship between the pursuit of pleasure and love? Apparently, both go together. Our virtues are based on pleasure, our morality is based on pleasure. We say you may come to it through sacrifice—which gives you pleasure!—or resistance, which might give you the pleasure of achieving something. So where is the line, if there is such a thing, between pleasure and love? Can the two go together, be interwoven? Or are they always separate? Man has said, 'Love God, and that love has nothing whatsoever to do with profane love'. You know this has been a problem not just for historical centuries, but right from the beginning of time. So where is the line that divides the two, or is there no line at all? One is not the other, and if we are pursuing pleasure, as most of us are—in the name of God, in the name of peace, in the name of social reform—then what place has love in this pursuit?

So one has to go into the questions: What is pleasure and what is enjoyment and what is joy? Is bliss related to pleasure? Don't say no or yes, let us find out. Look at a beautiful tree, a cloud, light on the water, a sunset, a vast expanse of sky, or the beautiful face of a man or a woman or a child. In the delight of seeing something really beautiful, there is great enjoyment, a real sense of appreciation of something extraordinary, noble, clear, lovely. And when you deny pleasure, you deny the whole perception of beauty. And religions have denied it. It is only quite recently, I've been told, that landscape painting came into religious paintings in the Western world, although in China and the East painting of the landscape and the tree was considered noble and religious.

Why does the mind pursue pleasure? Not is it right or wrong, but what is the mechanism of this pleasure principle? If you say you agree or disagree, then we are lost, but if we actually together find out what is the principle, the mechanism of this whole movement of pleasure, then perhaps we shall understand what is real enjoyment. Then what is joy and bliss, in which is involved ecstasy? Is ecstasy related to pleasure? Can joy ever become pleasure?

What is the mechanism of pleasure? Why does the mind pursue it so constantly? You cannot prevent perception—seeing a beautiful house, or a lovely green lawn and the sunshine on it, or the vast desert without a single blade of grass, and the expanse of the sky. You can't prevent seeing it, and the very seeing is pleasure, is a delight, isn't it? When you see a lovely face—not just a symmetrical face but one with depth in it, beauty, a quality behind it, intelligence, vitality—to see such a face is a marvel and in that perception there is a delight. Now, when does that delight become pleasure? You see a lovely statue by Michelangelo, and you look at it; it is the most extraordinary thing, not the subject, but the quality of it. In the perception of it, there is great pleasure, great delight.

You go away and the mind thinks about it, thought begins. You say what a lovely thing that was. In seeing, there was great feeling, a quality of perception of something marvellous; then thought recollects it, remembers it, and remembers the pleasure that you had when you saw that statue. Thought then creates that pleasure; it gives vitality, continuity, to that event which took place when you saw that statue. So thought is responsible for the pursuing of pleasure. It is not my invention, you can watch it. You see a lovely sunset, and later you say, 'I wish I could go back there and see it again'. At the moment of seeing that sunset, there was no pleasure. You saw something extraordinary, full of light and colour and depth. When you go away and go back to your life, your mind says, 'What a marvellous thing that was, I wish that I could have it repeated again'. So thought perpetuates that thing as pleasure. Is that the mechanism? Then what takes place? You never again see the sunset—*never!*—because the remembrance of that original sunset remains, and you always compare with that. Therefore you never again see something totally new.

So one asks: Can you see that sunset, or the beautiful face, or your sexual experience, or whatever it be, see it and finish it, not carry it over—whether that thing was great beauty or great sorrow or great physical or psychological pain? Can you see the beauty of it and be finished, completely finished, not take it over and store it up for the next day, next month, the future? If you do store it up, then thought plays with it. Thought is the storing up of that incident or that pain or that suffering or that thing that gave delight. So how is one not to prevent, but to be aware of this whole process and not let thought come into operation at all?

I *want* to see the sunset, I *want* to look at the trees, full of the beauty of the earth. It is not my earth or your earth, it is ours; it is not the Englishman's earth or the Russian's or the Indian's, it is our earth to live on, without all the frontiers, without all the ugly, beastly wars, and mischief of man. I want to look at all this. Have you ever seen palm trees on a solitary hill? What a marvellous thing it is! Or a single tree in a field? I *want* to look at it, I *want* to enjoy it, but I don't want to reduce it to an ugly little pleasure. And thought will reduce it.

How can thought function when necessary and not function at all in other directions? It is possible only when there is real awareness, awareness of the whole mechanism of thought, the structure and the nature of thought, where it must function—absolutely logically, healthily, not neurotically or personally—and where it has no place at all. So what are beauty and thought? Can the intellect ever perceive beauty? It may describe, it may imitate, it may copy, it may do many things, but the description is not the described. We could go on and on into this infinitely.

So when one understands the nature of pleasure and the principle of pleasure, then what is love? Is love jealousy? Is love possessiveness? Is love domination, attachment? You know all the business that goes on in life—the woman dominates the man or the man dominates the woman. The man does something because he wants to pursue it; he is ambitious, greedy, envious; he wants a position, prestige. His wife says, 'For God's sake, stop all that tommyrot and lead a different kind of life'. So there is a division between the two—even though they may sleep together. Can there be love when there is ambition, when each is pursuing his or her own particular private pleasures?

Then what is love? Obviously, it can only happen when there are no longer all the things that are not love, like ambition, competition, wanting to become somebody. That is our life: We want to be somebody famous, to fulfil, know, become a writer, an artist, something bigger. All that is what we want. Can such a man or woman know what love is? That means, can there be love for a man who is working for himself, not only in a little way, but in identifying himself with the state, with God, with social activity, with the country, with a series of beliefs? Obviously not. And yet that is the trap in which we are caught. Can we be aware of that trap, really aware—not because somebody describes it—be aware of the trap in which we are caught and break the trap? That's where the real revolution is, not the folly of revolutions of bombs and social changes. Though the social changes are necessary, the bombs are not.

So one discovers or one comes upon unknowingly, without inviting it, this thing called love when the other things are not. It happens when we have really understood the nature of pleasure and how thought destroys the thing that was a great joy. Joy cannot possibly be made into pleasure. Joy comes naturally; it happens; like happiness it comes. But the moment you say, 'Oh I am very happy', you are no longer happy.

Then what is love in human relationship? What is the place of love in human relationship? Has it any place at all? Yet we have to live together, we have to co-operate together, we have to have children together. Can the man who loves send his son to war? It is your problem. You have children, and your education is preparing the children for war, to kill. Find out! So what is that love, and what is its relationship to our human existence? I think that question can only be answered—truly, not verbally or intellectually—when the whole principle of pleasure, and thought, and this becoming, is understood. Then you will find a totally different kind of relationship.

With Students at Rajghat School, 19 December 1952

WE WERE DISCUSSING the complex problem of love. I do not think we shall understand it until we understand an equally complex problem, which we call the mind. Have you noticed, when we are very young, how inquisitive we are? We want to know, we see many more things than older people. We observe, if we are at all awake, things that older people do not notice. The mind, when we are young, is much more alert, much more curious and wanting to know. That is why, when we are young, we learn so easily mathematics, geography. As we grow older, our minds become more and more crystallized, more and more heavy, more and more bulky. Have you noticed in older people how prejudiced they are? Their minds are fixed, they are not open, they approach everything from a fixed point of view. You are young now; but if you are not very watchful, you will also become like that.

Is it not then very important to understand the mind, and to see whether you cannot be supple, be capable of instant adjustments, of extraordinary capacities in every department of life, of deep research and understanding, instead of gradually becoming dull? Should you not know the ways of the mind, so as to understand the way of love? Because it is the mind that destroys love. Clever people, people who are cunning, do not know what love is because their minds are so sharp, because they are so clever, because they are so superficial—which means to be on the surface—and love is not a thing that exists on the surface.

What is the mind? I am not talking about the brain, the physical construction of the brain about which any physiologist will tell you. The brain is something which reacts to various nervous responses. But you are going to find out what the mind is. The mind says, 'I think; it is mine; it is yours; I am hurt; I am jealous; I love; I hate; I am an Indian; I am a Moslem; I believe in this; I do not believe in that; I know; you do not know; I respect; I despise; I want; I do not want'. What is this thing? Until you understand it—until you are familiar with the whole process of thinking, which is the mind—until you are aware of that, you will gradually, as you grow older, become hard, crystallized, dull, fixed in a certain pattern of thinking.

What is this thing that you call the mind? It is the way of thinking, the way you think. I am talking of your mind—not somebody else's mind and the way it would think—the way you feel, the way you look at trees, at a fish, at the fishermen, the way you consider the villager. That mind gradually becomes warped or fixed in a certain pattern. When you want something, when you desire, when you crave, when you want to be something, then you set a pattern; that is, your mind creates a pattern and gets caught. Your desire crystallizes your mind. Say, for example, I want to be a very rich man. The desire of wanting to be a wealthy man creates a pattern and my thinking then gets caught in it, and I can only think in those terms, and I cannot go beyond it. So the mind gets caught in it, gets crystallized in it, gets hard, dull. Or if I believe in something—in God, in a certain political system—the very belief begins to set the pattern, because that belief is the outcome of my desire and that desire strengthens the walls of the pattern. Gradually, my mind becomes dull, incapable of adjustment, of quickness, of sharpness, of clarity, because I am caught in the labyrinth of my own desires.

So until I really investigate this process of my mind, the ways I think, the ways I regard love, until I am familiar with my own ways of thinking, I cannot possibly find what love is. There will be no love when my mind desires certain facts of love, certain actions of it, and when I then imagine what love should be. Then I give certain motives to love. So, gradually, I create the pattern of action with regard to love. But it is not love; it is merely my desire of what love should be. Say, for example, I possess you as a wife or as a husband. Do you understand *possess?* You possess your sari or your coat. If somebody took them away, you would be angry, you would be anxious, you would be irritated. Why? Because you regard your sari or your coat as yours, your property; you possess it; because through possession you feel enriched. Through having many saris, many coats, you feel rich, not only physically rich but inwardly rich. So when somebody takes your coat away, you feel irritated because inwardly you are being deprived of that feeling of being rich, that feeling of possession. Owning creates a barrier, does it not, with regard to love? If I own you, possess you, is that love? I possess you as I possess a car, a coat, a sari, because in possessing, I feel very rich; I depend on it; it is very important to me inwardly. This owning, this possessing, this depending, is what we call love. But if you examine it, you will see that, behind it, the mind feels satisfied in possession. After all, when you possess a sari or many saris or a car or a house, inwardly it gives you a certain satisfaction, the feeling that it is yours.

So the mind desiring, wanting, creates a pattern, and in that pattern it gets caught, and so the mind grows weary, dull, stupid, thoughtless. The mind is the centre of that feeling of the 'mine', the feeling that I own something, that I am a big man, that I am a little man, that I am insulted, that I am flattered, that I am clever or that I am very beautiful or that I want to be ambitious or that I am the daughter of somebody or the son of somebody. That feeling of the 'me', the 'I', is the centre of the mind, is the mind itself. So the more the mind feels 'This is mine', and builds walls around the feeling that 'I am somebody', that 'I must be great', that 'I am a very clever man', or that 'I am very stupid or a dull man', the more it creates a pattern, the more and more it becomes enclosed, dull. Then it suffers; then there is pain in that enclosure.

Then it says, 'What am I to do?' Then it struggles to find something else instead of removing the walls that are enclosing it—by thought, by careful awareness, by going into it, by understanding it. It wants to take something from outside and then to close itself again. So gradually, the mind becomes a barrier to love. So without the understanding of life, of what the mind is, of the way of thinking, of the way from which there is action, we cannot possibly find what love is.

Is not the mind also an instrument of comparison? You say this is better than that; you compare yourself with somebody who is more beautiful, who is more clever. There is comparison when you say, 'I remember that particular river that I saw a year ago, and it was still more beautiful'. You compare yourself with somebody, compare yourself with an example, with the ultimate ideal. Comparative judgment makes the mind dull; it does not sharpen the mind, it does not make the mind comprehensive, inclusive, because, when you are all the time comparing, what has happened? You see the sunset, and you immediately compare that sunset with the previous sunset. You see a mountain and you see how beautiful it is. Then you say, 'I saw a still more beautiful mountain two years ago'. When you are comparing, you are really not looking at the sunset which is there, but you are looking at it in order to compare it with something else. So comparison prevents you from looking fully. I look at you, you are nice, but I say, 'I know a much nicer person, a much better person, a more noble person, a more stupid person'. When I do this, I am not looking at you. Because my mind is occupied with something else, I am not looking at you at all. In the same way, I am not looking at the sunset at all. To really look at the sunset, there must be no comparison; to really look at you, I must not compare you with someone else. It is only when I look at you without comparative judgment that I can understand you. But when I compare you with somebody else, then I judge you and I say, 'Oh, he is a very stupid man'. So stupidity arises when there is comparison. I compare you with somebody else, and that very comparison brings about a lack of human dignity. When I look at you without comparing, I am only concerned with you, not with someone else. The very concern about you, not comparatively, brings about human dignity.

So as long as the mind is comparing, there is no love, and the mind is always judging, comparing, weighing, looking to find out where the weakness is. So where there is comparison, there is no love. When the mother and father love their children, they do not compare them, they do not compare their child with another child; it is their child and they love their child. But you want to compare yourself with something better, with something nobler, with something richer, so you create in yourself a lack of love. You are always concerned with yourself in relationship to somebody else. As the mind becomes more and more comparative, more and more possessive, more and more depending, it creates a pattern in which it gets caught, so it cannot look at anything anew, afresh. And so it destroys that very thing, that very perfume of life, which is love.

Student: Is there not an end of love? Is love based on attraction?

Krishnamurti: Suppose you are attracted by a beautiful river, by a beautiful woman, or by a man. What is wrong with that? We are trying to find out. You see, when I am attracted to a woman, to a man, or to a child or to truth, I want to be with it, I want to possess it, I want to call it my own; I say that it is mine and that it is not yours. I am attracted to that person, I must be near that person, my body must be near that person's body. So what have I done? What generally happens? The fact is that I am attracted and I want to be near that person; that is a fact, not an ideal. And it is also a fact that when I am attracted and I want to possess, there is no love. My concern is with the fact and not with what I should be. When I possess a person, I do not want that person to look at anybody else. When I consider that person as mine, is there love? Obviously not. The moment my mind creates a hedge round that person, as 'mine', there is no love.

The fact is, my mind is doing that all the time. That is what we are discussing, to see how the mind is working; and perhaps, being aware of it, the mind itself will be quiet.

S: Why does one feel the necessity of love?

K: You mean, why do we have to have love? Why should there be love? Can we do without it? What would happen if you did not have this so-called love? If your parents began to think out why they love you, you might not be here. They might throw you out. They think they love you; therefore they want to protect you, they want to see you educated, they feel that they must give you every opportunity to be something. This feeling of protection, this feeling of wanting you to be educated, this feeling that you belong to them, is what they generally call love. Without it, what would happen? What would happen if your parents did not love you? You would be neglected, you would be something inconvenient, you would be pushed out, they would hate you. So, fortunately, there is this feeling of love, perhaps clouded, perhaps besmirched and ugly, but there is still that feeling, fortunately for you and me; otherwise you and I would not have been educated, would not exist.

Bombay, 12 February 1950

Questioner: Our lives are empty of any real impulse of kindness, and we seek to fill this void with organized charity and compulsive justice. Sex is our life. Can you throw any light on this weary subject?

Krishnamurti: To translate the question: Our problem is that our lives are empty, and we know no love; we know sensations, we know advertising, we know sexual demands, but there is no love. And how is this emptiness to be transformed, how is one to find that flame without smoke? Surely, that is the question, is it not? So let us find out the truth of the matter together.

Why are our lives empty? Though we are very active, though we write books and go to cinemas, though we play, love, and go to the office, yet our lives are empty, boring, mere routine. Why are our relationships so tawdry, empty, and without much significance? We know our own lives sufficiently well to be aware that our existence has very little meaning; we quote phrases and ideas that we have learned—what so and so has said, what the mahatmas, the latest saints, or the ancient saints, have said. If it is not a religious, it is a political or intellectual leader that we follow, either Marx, or Adler, or Christ. We are just gramophone records repeating, and we call this repetition *knowledge*. We learn, we repeat, and our lives remain utterly tawdry, boring, and ugly. Why? Why is it like that? Why is it that we have given so much significance to the things of the mind? Why has the mind become so important in our lives?—mind being ideas, thought, the capacity to rationalize, to weigh, to balance, to calculate? Why have we given such extraordinary significance to the mind?—which does not mean that we must become emotional, sentimental, and gushy. We know this emptiness, we know this extraordinary sense of frustration. Why is there in our lives this vast shallowness, this sense of negation? Surely, we can understand it only when we approach it through awareness in relationship.

What is actually taking place in our relationships? Are not our relationships a self-isolation? Is not every activity of the mind a process of safeguarding, of seeking security, isolation? Is not that very thinking, which we say is collective, a process of isolation? Is not every action of our life a self-enclosing process? You can see it in your daily life. The family has become a self-isolating process, and being isolated, it must exist in opposition. So all our actions are leading to self-isolation, which creates this sense of emptiness; and being empty, we proceed to fill the emptiness with radios, with noise, with chatter, with gossip, with reading, with the acquisition of knowledge, with respectability, money, social position, and so on and on. But these are all part of the isolating process, and therefore they merely give strength to isolation. So for most of us, life is a process of isolation, of denial, resistance, conformity to a pattern; and naturally in that process there is no life, and therefore there is a sense of emptiness, a sense of frustration. Surely, to love someone is to be in communion with that person, not on one particular level, but completely, integrally, profusely; but we do not know such love. We know love only as sensation—my children, my wife, my property, my knowledge, my achievement; and that again is an isolating process. Our life in all directions leads to exclusion; it is a self-enclosing momentum of thought and feeling, and occasionally we have communion with another. That is why there is this enormous problem.

Now, that is the actual state of our lives—respectability, possession, and emptiness—and the question is how we are to go beyond it. How are we to go beyond this loneliness, this emptiness, this insufficiency, this inner poverty? I think most of us do not want to. Most of us are satisfied as we are; it is too tiresome to find out a new thing, so we prefer to remain as we are—and that is the real difficulty. We have so many securities; we have built walls around ourselves with which we are satisfied, and occasionally there is a whisper beyond the wall; occasionally there is an earthquake, a revolution, a disturbance which we soon smother. So most of us really do not want to go beyond the self-enclosing process; all we are seeking is a substitution, the same thing in a different form. Our dissatisfaction is so superficial; we want a new thing that will satisfy us, a new safety, a new way of protecting ourselves—which is again the process of isolation. We are actually seeking, not to go beyond isolation, but to strengthen isolation so that it will be permanent and undisturbed. It is only the very few who want to break through and see what is beyond this thing that we call emptiness, loneliness. Those who are seeking a substitution for the old will be satisfied by discovering something that offers a new security, but there are obviously some who will want to go beyond that, so let us proceed with them.

Now, to go beyond loneliness, emptiness, one must understand the whole process of the mind. What is this thing we call loneliness, emptiness? How do we know it is empty, how do we know it is lonely? By what measure do you say it is this and not that? When you say it is lonely, it is empty, what is the measure? You can know it only according to the measurement of the old. You say it is *empty*, you give it a name, and you think you have understood it. Is not the very naming of the thing a hindrance to the understanding of it? Most of us know what this loneliness is, from which we are trying to escape. Most of us are aware of this inner poverty, this inner insufficiency. It is not an abortive reaction, it is a fact, and by calling it some name, we cannot dissolve it—it is there. Now, how do we know its content, how do we know the nature of it? Do you know something by giving it a name? Do you know me by calling me by a name? You can know me only when you observe me, when you have communion with me, but calling me by a name, saying I am this or that, obviously puts an end to communion with me. Similarly, to know the nature of that thing which we call loneliness, there must be communion with it, and communion is not possible if you name it. To understand something, the naming must cease first. If you want to understand your child at all—which I doubt—what do you do? You look at him, watch him in his play, observe him, study him. In other words, you love that which you want to understand. When you love something, naturally there is communion with it, but love is not a word, a name, a thought. You cannot love that which you call *loneliness* because you are not fully aware of it, you approach it with fear—not fear of it, but of something else. You have not thought about loneliness because you do not really know what it is. Don't smile, this is not a clever argument. Experience the thing while we are talking, then you will see the significance of it.

So that thing that we call *the empty* is a process of isolation, which is the product of everyday relationship, because in relationship we are consciously or unconsciously seeking exclusion. You want to be the exclusive owner of your property, of your wife or husband, of your children; you want to name the thing or the person as *mine*, which obviously means exclusive acquisition. This process of exclusion must inevitably lead to a sense of isolation, and as nothing can live in isolation, there is conflict, and from that conflict we are trying to escape. All forms of escape of which we can possibly conceive—whether social activities, drink, the pursuit of God, *puja*, the performance of ceremonies, dancing, and other amusements—are on the same level; and if we see in daily life this total process of escape from conflict and want to go beyond it, we must understand relationship. It is only when the mind is not escaping in any form that it is possible to be in direct communion with that thing which we call loneliness, the alone, and to have communion with that thing, there must be affection, there must be love. In other words, you must love the thing to understand it. Love is the only revolution, and love is not a theory, not an idea; it does not follow any book or any pattern of social behaviour.

So the solution of the problem is not to be found in theories, which merely create further isolation. It is to be found only when the mind, which is thought, is not seeking an escape from loneliness. Escape is a process of isolation, and the truth of the matter is that there can be communion only when there is love. It is only then that the problem of loneliness is resolved.

Ojai, 28 August 1949

Questioner: Ideas do separate, but ideas also bring people together. Is this not the expression of love which makes communal life possible?

Krishnamurti: I wonder, when you ask such a question, whether you realize that ideas, beliefs, opinions, separate people; that ideologies break up; that ideas inevitably disrupt? Ideas do not hold people together—though you may try to bring together people belonging to differing and opposed ideologies. Ideas can never bring people together, because ideas can always be opposed and destroyed through conflict. After all, ideas are images, sensations, words. Can words, sensations, thoughts, bring people together? Or does one require quite a different thing to bring people together? One sees that hate, fear, and nationalism bring people together. Fear brings people together. A common hatred sometimes brings together people opposed to one another, as nationalism brings together people of opposing groups. Surely, these are ideas. And is love an idea? Can you think about love? You are able to think about a person whom you love, or the group of people whom you love. But is that love? When there is thought about love, is that love? Is thought love? And, surely, only love can bring people together, not thought—not one group in opposition to another group. Where love is, there is no group, no class, no nationality. So one has to find out what we mean by love.

We know what we mean by ideas, opinions, beliefs. So what do we mean by love? Is it a thing of the mind? It is a thing of the mind, when the things of the mind fill the heart. And with most of us, it is so. We have filled our heart with the things of the mind, which are opinions, ideas, sensations, beliefs; and around that and in that we live and love. But is that love? Can we think about love? When you love, is thought functioning? Love and thought are not in opposition; do not let us divide them as opposites. When one loves, is there a sense of separateness, of bringing people together, or disbanding them, pushing them away? Surely that state of love can be experienced only when the process of thought is not functioning—which does not mean that one must become crazy, unbalanced. On the contrary. It requires the highest form of thought to go beyond.

So love is not a thing of the mind. It is only when the mind is really quiet, when it is no longer expecting, asking, demanding, seeking, possessing, being jealous, fearful, anxious—when the mind is really silent, only then is there a possibility of love. When the mind is no longer projecting itself, pursuing its particular sensations, demands, urges, hidden fears, no longer seeking self-fulfilment or being held in bondage to belief—only then is there a possibility of love. But most of us think love can go with jealousy, with ambition, with the pursuit of personal desires and ambitions. Surely, when these things exist, love is not.

So we must be concerned not with love, which comes into being spontaneously, without our particularly seeking it, but we must be concerned with the things that are hindering love, with the things of the mind which project themselves and create a barrier. And that is why it is important, before we can know what love is, to know what is the process of the mind, which is the seat of the self. And that is why it is important to go ever more deeply into the question of self-knowledge—not merely say, 'I must love', or 'Love brings people together', or 'Ideas disrupt', which would be a mere repetition of what you have heard, therefore utterly useless. Words entangle. But if one can understand the whole significance of the ways of one's thought, the ways of our desires and their pursuits and ambitions, then there is a possibility of having or understanding that which is love. But that requires an extraordinary understanding of oneself.

When there is self-abnegation, when there is self-forgetfulness—not intentionally, but spontaneously, a self-forgetfulness, self-denial that is not the outcome of practices or disciplines that merely limit—then there is a possibility of love. That self-denial comes into being when the whole process of the self is understood, consciously as well as unconsciously, in the waking hours as well as in dreaming. Then the total process of the mind is understood as it is actually taking place in relationship, in every incident, in every response to every challenge that one has. In understanding that, and therefore freeing the mind from its own self-correcting, self-limiting process, there is a possibility of love.

Love is not sentiment, not romanticism, not dependent on something, and that state is extremely arduous and difficult to understand, or to be in—because our minds are always interfering, limiting, encroaching upon its functioning. Therefore it is important to understand first the mind and its ways; otherwise we shall be caught in illusions, caught in words and sensations that have very little significance. For most people, ideas merely act as a refuge, as an escape; ideas which have become beliefs naturally prevent complete living, complete action, right thinking. It is possible to think rightly, to live freely and intelligently, only when there is ever deeper and wider self-knowledge.

Bombay, 12 March 1950

Questioner: We know sex as an inescapable physical and psychological necessity, and it seems to be a root cause of chaos in the personal life of our generation. It is a horror to young women who are victims of men's lust. Suppression and indulgence are equally ineffective. How can we deal with this problem?

Krishnamurti: Why is it that whatever we touch we turn into a problem? We have made God a problem, we have made love a problem, we have made relationship, living, a problem, and we have made sex a problem. Why? Why is everything we do a problem, a horror? Why are we suffering? Why has sex become a problem? Why do we submit to living with problems; why do we not put an end to them? Why do we not die to our problems instead of carrying them day after day, year after year? Surely, sex is a relevant question, but there is the primary question: Why do we make life into a problem? Working, sex, earning money, thinking, feeling, experiencing—you know, the whole business of living—why is it a problem? Is it not essentially because we always think from a particular point of view, from a fixed point of view? We are always thinking from a centre towards the periphery, but the periphery is the centre for most of us, and so anything we touch is superficial. But life is not superficial; it demands living completely. And because we are living only superficially, we know only superficial reaction. Whatever we do on the periphery must inevitably create a problem, and that is our life—we live in the superficial, and we are content to live there with all the problems of the superficial.

So problems exist as long as we live in the superficial, on the periphery—the periphery being the 'me' and its sensations, which can be externalized or made subjective, which can be identified with the universe, with the country, or with some other thing made up by the mind. So as long as we live within the field of the mind, there must be complications, there must be problems, and that is all we know. Mind is sensation, mind is the result of accumulated sensations and reactions, and anything it touches is bound to create misery, confusion, an endless problem. The mind is the real cause of our problems, the mind that is working mechanically night and day, consciously and unconsciously. The mind is a most superficial thing, and we have spent generations—we spend our whole lives—cultivating the mind, making it more and more clever, more and more subtle, more and more cunning, more and more dishonest and crooked—all of which is apparent in every activity of our life. The very nature of our mind is to be dishonest, crooked, incapable of facing facts, and that is the thing that creates problems, that is the thing which is the problem itself.

Now, what do we mean by the problem of sex? Is it the act, or is it a thought about the act? Surely, it is not the act. The sexual act is no problem to you, any more than eating is a problem to you; but if you think about eating all day long because you have nothing else to think about, it becomes a problem to you. So is the sexual act the problem, or is it the thought about the act? Why do you think about it? Why do you build it up? The cinemas, the magazines, the stories, the way people dress, everything is building up your thought of sex. Why does the mind build it up; why does the mind think about sex at all? Why has it become a central issue in your life? When there are so many things calling, demanding your attention, you give complete attention to the thought of sex. Why is your mind so occupied with it? Because that is a way of ultimate escape. It is a way of complete self-forgetfulness. For the time being, at least for that moment, you can forget yourself—and there is no other way of forgetting yourself. Everything else you do in life gives emphasis to the 'me', to the self. Your business, your religion, your gods, your leaders, your political and economic actions, your escapes, your social activities, your joining one party and rejecting another—all that is emphasizing and giving strength to the 'me'. That is, there is only one act in which there is no emphasis on the 'me', so it becomes a problem. When there is only one thing in your life that is an avenue to ultimate escape, to complete forgetfulness of yourself if only for a few seconds, you cling to it because that is the only moment you are happy. Every other issue you touch becomes a nightmare, a source of suffering and pain, so you cling to the one thing that gives complete self-forgetfulness, which you call happiness. But when you cling to it, it too becomes a nightmare, because then you want to be free from it; you do not want to be a slave to it. So you invent, again from the mind, the idea of chastity, of celibacy, and you try to be celibate, to be chaste, through suppression, denial, meditation, through all kinds of religious practices, all of which are operations of the mind to cut itself off from the fact. This again gives particular emphasis to the 'me', who is trying to become something; so again you are caught in travail, in trouble, in effort, in pain.

So sex becomes an extraordinarily difficult and complex problem as long as you do not understand the mind which thinks about the problem. The act itself can never be a problem, but the thought about the act creates the problem. You safeguard the act; you live loosely or indulge yourself in marriage. Surely, the problem can be solved only when you understand the whole process and structure of the 'me' and the 'mine': my wife, my husband, my child, my property, my car, my achievement, my success; and until you understand and resolve all that, sex as a problem will remain. As long as you are ambitious—politically, religiously, or in any way—as long as you are emphasizing the self, the thinker, the experiencer, by feeding it on ambition, whether in the name of yourself as an individual or in the name of the country, of the party, or of an idea which you call religion, as long as there is this activity of self-expansion, you will have a sexual problem.

Surely, you are creating, feeding, expanding yourself on the one hand, and on the other you are trying to forget yourself, to lose yourself if only for a moment. How can the two exist together? So your life is a contradiction: emphasis on the 'me', and forgetting the 'me'. Sex is not a problem; the problem is this contradiction in your life, and the contradiction cannot be bridged over by the mind, because the mind itself is a contradiction. The contradiction can be understood only when you understand fully the whole process of your daily existence. Going to the cinemas, reading books which stimulate thought, the magazines with their half-naked pictures, your way of looking at others, the surreptitious eyes that catch you—all these things are encouraging the mind through devious ways to emphasize the self; and, at the same time, you try to be kind, loving, tender. The two cannot go together.

The man who is ambitious, spiritually or otherwise, can never be without a problem, because problems cease only when the self is forgotten, when the 'me' is non-existent; and that state of the non-existence of the self is not an act of will, it is not a mere reaction. Sex becomes a reaction, and when the mind tries to solve the problem, it only makes the problem more confused, more troublesome, more painful. So the act is not the problem, but the mind is the problem—the mind that says it must be chaste. Chastity is not of the mind. The mind can only suppress its own activities, and suppression is not chastity. Chastity is not a virtue, chastity cannot be cultivated. The man who is cultivating humility is surely not a humble man; he may call his pride humility, but he is a proud man, and that is why he seeks to become humble. Pride can never become humble, and chastity is not a thing of the mind—you cannot *become* chaste. You will know chastity only when there is love, and love is not of the mind nor a thing of the mind.

So the problem of sex, which tortures so many people all over the world, cannot be resolved until the mind is understood. We cannot put an end to thinking, but thought comes to an end when the thinker ceases, and the thinker ceases only when there is an understanding of the whole process. Fear comes into being when there is division between the thinker and his thought; when there is no thinker, then only is there no conflict in thought. What is implicit needs no effort to understand. The thinker comes into being through thought; then the thinker exerts himself to shape, to control his thoughts, or to put an end to them. The thinker is a fictitious entity, an illusion of the mind. When there is a realization of thought as a fact, then there is no need to think about the fact. If there is simple, choiceless awareness, then that which is implicit in the fact begins to reveal itself. Therefore thought as fact ends. Then you will see that the problems which are eating at our hearts and minds, the problems of our social structure, can be resolved. Then sex is no longer a problem, it has its proper place, it is neither an impure thing nor a pure thing.

Sex has its place, but when the mind gives it the predominant place, then it becomes a problem. The mind gives sex a predominant place because it cannot live without some happiness, and so sex becomes a problem; but when the mind understands its whole process and so comes to an end, that is, when thinking ceases, then there is creation, and it is that creation which makes us happy. To be in that state of creation is bliss, because it is self-forgetfulness in which there is no reaction as from the self. This is not an abstract answer to the daily problem of sex—it is the only answer. The mind denies love, and without love there is no chastity. It is because there is no love that you make sex into a problem.

Q: Love, as we know and experience it, is a fusion between two people, or between the members of a group; it is exclusive, and in it there is both pain and joy. When you say love is the only solvent of life's problems, you are giving a connotation to the word which we have hardly experienced. Can a common man like me ever know love in your sense?

K: Everybody can know love, but you can know it only when you are capable of looking at facts very clearly, without resistance, without justification, without explaining them away—just look at things closely, observe them very clearly and minutely. Now, what is the thing that we call love? The questioner says that it is exclusive, and that in it we know pain and joy. Is love exclusive? We shall find out when we examine what we call love, what the so-called common man calls love. There is no common man. There is only man, which is you and I. The common man is a fictitious entity invented by the politicians. There is only man, which is you and I who are in sorrow, in pain, in anxiety, and fear.

Now, what is our life? To find out what love is, let us begin with what we know. What is our love? In the midst of pain and pleasure, we know it is exclusive, personal: my wife, my children, my country, my God. We know it as a flame in the midst of smoke, we know it through jealousy, we know it through domination, we know it through possession, we know it through loss when the other is gone. So we know love as sensation, do we not? When we say we love, we know jealousy, we know fear, we know anxiety. When you say you love someone, all that is implied: envy, the desire to possess, the desire to own, to dominate, the fear of loss, and so on. All this we call love, and we do not know love without fear, without envy, without possession; we merely verbalize that state of love which is without fear; we call it impersonal, pure, divine, or God knows what else, but the fact is that we are jealous, we are dominating, possessive. We shall know that state of love only when jealousy, envy, possessiveness, domination, come to an end; and as long as we possess, we shall never love.

Envy, possession, hatred, the desire to dominate the person or the thing called *mine*, the desire to possess and to be possessed—all that is a process of thought, is it not? Is love a process of thought? Is love a thing of the mind? Actually, for most of us, it is. Do not say it is not—it is nonsense to say that. Do not deny the fact that your love is a thing of the mind. Surely it is; otherwise, you would not possess, you would not dominate, you would not say, 'It is mine'. Since you do say it, your love is a thing of the mind; so love, for you, is a process of thought. You can think about the person whom you love, but is thinking about the person whom you love, love? When do you think about the person whom you love? You think about her when she is gone, when she is away, when she has left you. But when she no longer disturbs you, when you can say, 'She is mine', then you do not have to think about her. You do not have to think about your furniture, it is part of you—which is a process of identification so as not to be disturbed, to avoid trouble, anxiety, sorrow. So you miss the person whom you say you love only when you are disturbed, when you are in suffering; and as long as you possess that person, you do not have to think about that person, because in possession there is no disturbance. But when possession is disturbed, you begin to think, and then you say, 'I love that person'. So your love is merely a reaction of the mind, is it not?—which means your love is merely a sensation, and sensation is surely not love. Do you think about the person when you are close? When you possess, hold, dominate, control, when you can say, 'She is mine' or 'He is mine', there is no problem. As long as you are certain in your possession, there is no problem. And society, everything you have built around you, helps you to possess so as not to be disturbed, so as not to think about it. Thinking comes when you are disturbed—and you are bound to be disturbed as long as your thinking is what you call *love*.

Surely, love is not a thing of the mind. It is because the things of the mind have filled our hearts that we have no love. The things of the mind are jealousy, envy, ambition, the desire to be somebody, to achieve success. These things of the mind fill your heart, and then you say you love; but how can you love when you have all these confusing elements in you? When there is smoke, how can there be a pure flame? Love is not a thing of the mind, and love is the only solution to our problems. Love is not of the mind, and the man who has accumulated money or knowledge can never know love, because he lives with the things of the mind; his activities are of the mind, and whatever he touches he makes into a problem, a confusion, a misery.

So what we call our love is a thing of the mind. Look at yourself and you will see that what I am saying is obviously true;

otherwise our lives, our marriages, our relationships, would be entirely different; we would have a new society. We bind ourselves to another, not through fusion, but through contract, which is called love, marriage. Love does not fuse, adjust—it is neither personal nor impersonal; it is a state of being. The man who desires to fuse with something greater, to unite himself with another, is avoiding misery, confusion; but the mind is still in separation, which is disintegration. Love knows neither fusion nor diffusion; it is neither personal nor impersonal; it is a state of being which the mind cannot find—it can describe it, give it a term, a name, but the word, the description, is not love.

It is only when the mind is quiet that it shall know love, and that state of quietness is not a thing to be cultivated. Cultivation is still the action of the mind; discipline is still a product of the mind, and a mind that is disciplined, controlled, subjugated, a mind that is resisting, explaining, cannot know love. You may read, you may listen to what is being said about love, but that is not love. Only when you put away the things of the mind, only when your heart is empty of the things of the mind, is there love. Then you will know what it is to love without separation, without distance, without time, without fear—and that is not reserved to the few. Love knows no hierarchy; there is only love. There are the many and the one, an exclusiveness, only when you do not love. When you love, there is neither the 'you' nor the 'me'. In that state there is only a flame without smoke.

New York, 18 June 1950

Questioner: How am I to get rid of fear, which influences all my activities?

Krishnamurti: This is a very complex question requiring close attention. And if we do not follow and explore it fully, in the sense of experiencing each step as we go along, we will not be able at the end of it to be free of fear.

What do we mean by fear? Fear of what? There are various types of fear, and we need not analyse every type. But we can see that fear comes into being when our comprehension of relationship is not complete. Relationship is not only between people, but between ourselves and nature, between ourselves and property, between ourselves and ideas; and as long as that relationship is not fully understood, there must be fear. Life is relationship. To be, is to be related, and without relationship there is no life. Nothing can exist in isolation, and as long as the mind is seeking isolation, there must be fear. So fear is not an abstraction; it exists only in relation to something.

Now, the question is how to be rid of fear. First of all, anything that is overcome has to be conquered again and again. No problem can be finally overcome, conquered; it can be understood, but not conquered. They are two completely different processes, and the conquering process leads to further confusion, further fear.

To resist, to dominate, to do battle with a problem, or to build a defence against it, is only to create further conflict. Whereas if we can understand fear, go into it fully step by step, explore the whole content of it, then fear will never return in any form—and that is what I hope we can do now.

As I said, fear is not an abstraction; it exists only in relationship. Now, what do we mean by fear? Ultimately, we are afraid of not being, of not becoming. Now, when there is fear of not being, of not advancing, or fear of the unknown, of death, can that fear be overcome by determination, by a conclusion, by any choice? Obviously not. Mere suppression, sublimation, or substitution creates further resistance, does it not? So fear can never be overcome through any form of discipline, through any form of resistance. Nor can there be freedom from fear through the search for an answer, or through mere intellectual or verbal explanation.

Now, what are we afraid of? Are we afraid of a fact, or of an idea about the fact? Please see this point. Are we afraid of the thing as it is, or are we afraid of what we think it is? Take death, for example. Are we afraid of the fact of death, or of the idea of death? The fact is one thing, and the idea about the fact is another. Am I afraid of the word *death*, or of the fact itself? Because I am afraid of the word, of the idea, I never understand the fact, I never look at the fact, I am never in direct relation with the fact. It is only when I am in complete communion with the fact that there is no fear. But if I am not in communion with the fact, then there is fear, and there is no communion with the fact as long as I have an idea, an opinion, a theory, about the fact. So I have to be very clear whether I am afraid of the word, the idea, or of the fact. If I am face to face with the fact, there is nothing to understand about it, the fact is there, and I can deal with it. But if I am afraid of the word, then I must understand the word, go into the whole process of what the word implies.

For example, one is afraid of loneliness, afraid of the ache, the pain of loneliness. Surely, that fear exists because one has never really looked at loneliness, one has never been in complete communion with it. The moment one is completely open to the fact of loneliness, one can understand what it is; but one has an idea, an opinion about it, based on previous knowledge, and it is this idea, opinion, this previous knowledge about the fact, that creates fear. So fear is obviously the outcome of naming, of terming, of projecting a symbol to represent the fact; that is, fear is not independent of the word.

I have a reaction, say, to loneliness; that is, I say I am afraid of being nothing. Am I afraid of the fact itself, or is that fear awakened because I have previous knowledge of the fact, knowledge being the word, the symbol, the image? How can there be fear of a fact? When I am face to face with a fact, in direct communion with it, I can look at it, observe it; therefore there is no fear of the fact. What causes fear is my apprehension about the fact, what the fact might be or do.

So it is my opinion, my idea, my experience, my knowledge about the fact, that creates fear. As long as there is verbalization of the fact—giving the fact a name and therefore identifying or condemning it—as long as thought is judging the fact as an observer, there must be fear. Thought is the product of the past; it can only exist through verbalization, through symbols, through images; and as long as thought is regarding or translating the fact, there must be fear.

So it is the mind that creates fear, the mind being the process of thinking. Thinking is verbalization. You cannot think without words, without symbols, images; these images, which are the prejudices, the previous knowledge, the apprehensions of the mind, are projected upon the fact, and out of that there arises fear. There is freedom from fear only when the mind is capable of looking at the fact without translating it, without giving it a name, a label. This is quite difficult, because the feelings, the reactions, the anxieties that we have, are promptly identified by the mind and given a word. The feeling of jealousy is identified by that word. Now, is it possible not to identify a feeling, to look at that feeling without naming it? It is the naming of the feeling that gives it continuity, that gives it strength. The moment you give a name to that which you call fear you strengthen it, but if you can look at that feeling without terming it, you will see that it withers away. Therefore, if one would be completely free of fear, it is essential to understand this whole process of terming, of projecting symbols, images, giving names to facts. That is, there can be freedom from fear only when there is self-knowledge. Self-knowledge is the beginning of wisdom, which is the ending of fear.

Q: How can I permanently get rid of sexual desire?

K: Why do we want to get permanently rid of a desire? You call it sexual, somebody else calls it attachment, fear, and so on. Why do we want to get rid of any desire permanently? Because that particular desire is disturbing to us, and we don't want to be disturbed. That is our whole process of thinking, is it not? We want to be self-enclosed, without any disturbance. That is, we want to be isolated, but nothing can live in isolation. In his search for God, the so-called religious person is really seeking complete isolation, in which he will never be disturbed; but such a person is not really religious. The truly religious are those who understand relationship completely, fully, and therefore have no problems, no conflict. Not that they are not disturbed, but because they are not seeking certainty, they understand disturbance, and therefore there is no self-enclosing process created by the desire for security.

Now, this question requires a great deal of understanding, because we are dealing with sensation, which is thought. To most people, sex has become an extraordinarily important problem. People being uncreative, afraid, enclosed, cut off in all other directions, sex is the only thing through which they can find a release, the one act in which the self is momentarily absent. In that brief state of abnegation when the self, the 'me', with all its troubles, confusions, and worries, is absent, there is great happiness. Through self-forgetfulness there is a sense of quietness, a release, and because we are uncreative religiously, economically, and in every other direction, sex becomes an overwhelmingly important problem. In daily life we are mere gramophone records, repeating phrases that we have learned; religiously we are automatons, mechanically following the priest; economically and socially we are bound, strangled, by environmental influences. Is there a release for us in any of that? Obviously not; and where there is no release, there must be frustration. That is why the sexual act, in which there is a release, has become such a vital problem for most of us. And society encourages and stimulates it through advertisements, magazines, the cinema, and all the rest of it.

As long as the mind, which is the result, the focal point of sensation, regards sex as a means of its release, sex must be a problem, and that problem will continue as long as we are incapable of being creative comprehensively, totally, and not merely in one particular direction. Creativeness has nothing to do with sensation. Sex is of the mind, and creation is not of the mind. Creation is never a product of the mind, a product of thought, and in that sense, sex, which is sensation, can never be creative. It may produce babies, but that is obviously not creativeness. As long as we depend for release on sensation, on stimulation in any form, there must be frustration, because the mind becomes incapable of realizing what creativeness is.

This problem cannot be resolved by any discipline, by any taboos, by any social edicts or sanctions. It can be resolved only when we understand the whole process of the mind, because it is the mind that is sexual. It is the mind's images, fancies, and pictures that stimulate it to be sexual, and as the mind is the result of sensation, it can only become more and more sensuous. Such a mind can never be creative because creation is not sensation. It is only when the mind does not seek stimuli in any form, whether outward or inward, that it can be completely quiet, free, and only in that freedom is there creation. We have made sex into something ugly because it is the only private sensation that we have; all other sensations are public, open. But as long as we use sensation in any form as a means of release, it will only increase the problems, the confusion and trouble, because release can never come into being through seeking a result.

The questioner wants to end sexual desire permanently because he has an idea that then he will be in a state in which all disturbances have disappeared; that is why he is seeking it, striving towards it. The very striving towards that state is preventing him from being free to understand the process of the mind. As long as the mind is merely seeking a permanent state in which it will have no disturbance of any kind, it is closed, and therefore it can never be creative. It is only when the mind is free of the desire to become something, to achieve a result, and hence free of fear, that it can be utterly quiet. Only then is there a possibility of that creativeness which is reality.

Q: I am not loved and I want to be, for without it life has no meaning. How can I fulfil this longing?

K: I hope you are not merely listening to words, because then they will be another distraction, a waste of time. But if you are really experiencing the things that we are discussing, then they will have an extraordinary significance; because though you may follow words with the conscious mind, if you are experiencing what is being said, the unconscious also takes part in it. Given an opportunity, the unconscious will reveal its whole content, and so bring about a complete understanding of ourselves. So I hope you are not merely listening to a talk, but are actually experiencing the things as we go along.

The questioner wants to know how to love and to be loved. Is not that the state of most of us? We all want to be loved, and also to give love. We talk a great deal about it. All religions, all preachers, talk about it. So let us find out what we mean by love.

Is love sensation? Is love a thing of the mind? Can you think about love? You can think about the object of love, but you cannot think about love, can you? I can think about the person I love; I can have a picture, an image of that person, and recall the sensations, the memories, of our relationship. But is love sensation, memory? When I say, 'I want to love and be loved', is that not merely thought, a reflection of the mind? Is thought love? We think it is, do we not? To us, love is sensation. That is why we have pictures of the people whom we love, that is why we think about them and are attached to them. That is all a process of thought, is it not?

Now, thought is frustrated in different directions, and therefore it says, 'I find happiness in love, so I must have love'. That is why we cling to the person we love; that is why we possess the person, psychologically as well as physiologically. We create laws to protect the possession of what we love, whether it be a person, a piano, a piece of property, or an idea, a belief, because in possession—with all its complications of jealousy, fear, suspicion, anxiety—we feel secure. So we have made love into a thing of the mind, and with the things of the mind we fill the heart. Because the heart is empty, the mind says, 'I must have that love', and we try to fulfil ourselves through the wife, through the husband. Through love we try to become something. That is, love becomes a useful thing; we use love as a means to an end.

So we have made of love a thing of the mind. The mind becomes the instrument of love, and the mind is only sensation. Thought is the reaction of memory to sensation. Without the symbol, the word, the image, there is no memory, there is no thought. We know the sensation of so-called love, and we cling to that, and when it fails we want some other expression of that same sensation. So the more we cultivate sensation, the more we cultivate so-called knowledge—which is merely memory—the less there is of love.

As long as we are seeking love, there must be a self-enclosing process. Love implies vulnerability, love implies communion, and there can be no communion, no vulnerability, as long as there is the self-enclosing process of thought. The very process of thought is fear, and how can there be communion with another when there is fear, when we use thought as a means for further stimulation?

There can be love only when you understand the whole process of the mind. Love is not of the mind, and you cannot think about love. When you say, 'I want love', you are thinking about it, you are longing for it, which is a sensation, a means to an end. Therefore it is not love that you want, but stimulation; you want a means through which you can fulfil yourself, whether it be a person, a job, or a particular excitement, and so on. Surely, that is not love. Love can be only when the thought of the self is absent, and freedom from the self lies through self-knowledge. With self-knowledge there comes understanding, and when the total process of the mind is completely and fully revealed and understood, then you will know what it is to love. Then you will see that love has nothing to do with sensation, that it is not a means of fulfilment. Then love is by itself, without any result. Love is a state of being, and in that state, the 'me', with its identifications, anxieties, and possessions, is absent. Love cannot be, as long as the activities of the self, of the 'me', whether conscious or unconscious, continue to exist. That is why it is important to understand the process of the self, the centre of recognition which is the 'me'.

Seattle, 6 August 1950

Questioner: How am I to overcome loneliness?

Krishnamurti: Can you overcome loneliness? Whatever you conquer has to be conquered again and again, does it not? What you understand comes to an end, but that which you conquer can never come to an end. The battling process only feeds and strengthens that with which you fight.

Now, what is this loneliness of which most of us are aware? We know it, and we run away from it, do we not? We take flight from it into every form of activity. We are empty, lonely, and we are afraid of it, so we try to cover it up by some means or other—meditation, the search for God, social activity, the radio, drink, or what you will—we would do anything else rather than face it, be with it, understand it. Running away is the same, whether we do it through the idea of God, or through drink. As long as one is escaping from loneliness, there is no essential difference between the worship of God and addiction to alcohol. Socially, there may be a difference; but psychologically, the man who runs away from himself, from his own emptiness, whose escape is his search for God, is on the same level as the drunkard.

What is important, then, is not to overcome loneliness, but to understand it, and we cannot understand it if we do not face it, if we do not look at it directly, if we are continually running away from it. And our whole life is a process of running away from loneliness, is it not? In relationship we use others to cover up loneliness; our pursuit of knowledge, our gathering of experience, everything we do, is a distraction, an escape from that emptiness. So these distractions and escapes must obviously come to an end. If we are to understand something, we must give our full attention to it. And how can we give full attention to loneliness if we are afraid of it, if we are running away from it through some distraction? So when we really want to understand loneliness, when our intention is to go fully, completely into it, because we see that there can be no creativeness as long as we do not understand that inward insufficiency which is the fundamental cause of fear—when we come to that point, then every form of distraction ends, does it not? Many people laugh at loneliness and say, 'Oh, that is only for the bourgeois; for God's sake, be occupied with something and forget it'. But emptiness cannot be forgotten, it cannot be put aside.

So if one would really understand this fundamental thing which we call loneliness, all escape must cease; but escape does not cease through worry, through seeking a result, or through any action of desire. One must see that without understanding loneliness every form of action is a distraction, an escape, a process of self-isolation, which only creates more conflict, more misery. To see that fact is essential, for only then can one face loneliness.

Then, if we go still more deeply into it, the problem arises of whether what we call loneliness is an actuality, or merely a word. Is loneliness an actuality, or merely a word which covers something that may not be what we think it is? Is not loneliness a thought, the result of thinking? That is, thinking is verbalization based on memory; don't we, with that verbalization, with that thought, with that memory, look at the state which we call *lonely?* So the very giving of a name to that state may be the cause of the fear which prevents us from looking at it more closely; and if we do not give it a name, which is fabricated by the mind, then is that state lonely?

Surely, there is a difference between loneliness and being alone. Loneliness is the ultimate in the process of self-isolation.

The more you are conscious of yourself, the more isolated you are, and self-consciousness is the process of isolation. But aloneness is not isolation. There is aloneness only when loneliness has come to an end. Aloneness is a state in which all influence has completely ceased, both the influence from outside, and the inner influence of memory; and only when the mind is in that state of aloneness can it know the incorruptible. But to come to that, we must understand loneliness, this process of isolation, which is the self and its activity. So the understanding of the self is the beginning of the cessation of isolation, and therefore of loneliness.

Madras, 3 February 1952

Questioner: How is man to fulfil himself if he has no ideals?

Krishnamurti: Is there such a thing as fulfilment, though most of us seek fulfilment? We know we try to fulfil ourselves through family, through son, through brother, through wife, through property, through identification with a country or a group, or through pursuit of an ideal, or through the desire for continuity of the 'me'. There are different forms of fulfilment at different levels of consciousness.

Is there such a thing as fulfilment? What is the thing that is fulfilling? What is the entity that is seeking to be, in or through certain identification? When do you think of fulfilment? When are you seeking fulfilment?

If you treat what we are saying at a verbal level, then go away, it is a waste of time. But if you want to go deeply, then pursue, then be alert and follow it, because we need intelligence, not dead repetition of phrases, words, and examples we are fed up with. What we need is creation, intelligent integrated creation; which means you have to search it out directly through your own understanding of the mind process. So in listening to what I am saying, relate it to yourself directly, experience what I am talking about. And you cannot experience it through my words. You can experience it only when you are capable, when you are earnest, when you observe your own thinking, your own feeling.

When is desire to be fulfilled? When are you conscious of this urge to be, to become, to fulfil? Please watch yourself. When are you conscious of it? Are you not conscious of it when you thwart it? Are you not aware of it when you feel extraordinary loneliness, a sense of inexhaustible nothingness, of yourself not being something. You are aware of this urge for fulfilment only when you feel an emptiness, loneliness. And then you pursue fulfilment through innumerable forms, through sex, through relationship with property, with trees, with everything at different layers of consciousness. The desire to be, to identify, to fulfil, exists only when there is consciousness of the 'me' being empty, lonely. The desire to fulfil is an escape from that which we call loneliness. So our problem is not how to fulfil, or what fulfilment is, because there is no such thing as fulfilment. The 'me' can never fulfil; it is always empty. You may have a few sensations when you are achieving a result, but the moment the sensations have gone you are back again in that empty state. So you begin to pursue the same process as before.

So the 'me' is the creator of that emptiness. The 'me' is the empty; the 'me' is a self-enclosing process in which we are aware of that extraordinary loneliness. So being aware of that, we are trying to run away through various forms of identification. These identifications we call fulfilments. Actually, there is no fulfilment because mind, the 'me', can never fulfil; it is the very nature of the 'me' to be self-enclosing.

So what is the mind which is aware of that emptiness to do? That is your problem, is it not? For most of us, this ache of emptiness is extraordinarily strong. We do anything to escape from it. Any illusion is sufficient, and that is the source of illusion. Mind has the power to create illusion. And as long as we do not understand that aloneness, that state of self-enclosing emptiness—do what you will, seek whatever fulfilment you will—there is always that barrier which divides, which knows no completeness.

So our difficulty is to be conscious of this emptiness, of this loneliness. We are never face to face with it. We do not know what it looks like, what its qualities are, because we are always running away from it, withdrawing, isolating, identifying. We are never face to face directly, in communion with it. We are the observer and the observed: That is, the mind, the 'I', observes that emptiness, and the 'I', the thinker, then proceeds to free itself from that emptiness or to run away.

So is that emptiness, loneliness, different from the observer? Isn't the observer himself empty? Because if the observer were not capable of recognizing that state which he calls loneliness, there would be no experience. He is empty; he cannot act upon it, he can do nothing about it. Because if he does anything whatsoever, he becomes the observer acting upon the observed, which is a false relationship.

So when the mind recognizes, realizes, is aware that it is empty and that it cannot act upon it, then that emptiness of which we are aware from outside has a different meaning. So far, we have approached it as the observer. Now, the observer himself is empty, alone, is lonely. Can he do anything about it? Obviously, he cannot. Then his relationship to it is entirely different from that of the relationship of the observer. He has that aloneness. He is in that state in which there is no verbalization that 'I am empty'. The moment he verbalizes it or externalizes it, he is different from that. So when verbalization ceases, when the experiencer ceases as experiencing loneliness, when he ceases to run away, then he is entirely lonely. His relationship is in itself loneliness; he is himself that, and when he realizes that fully, surely that emptiness, loneliness, ceases to be.

Loneliness is entirely different from aloneness. That loneliness must be passed to be alone. Loneliness is not comparable with aloneness. The man who knows loneliness can never know that which is alone. Are you in that state of aloneness? Our minds are not integrated to be alone. The very process of the mind is separative. And that which separates knows loneliness.

But aloneness is not separative. It is something that is not the many, not influenced by the many, not the result of the many, that is not put together as the mind is; the mind is of the many. Mind is not an entity that is alone, having been put together, brought together, manufactured, through centuries. Mind can never be alone. Mind can never know aloneness. But if you are aware of the loneliness when going through it, there comes into being that aloneness. Then only can there be that which is immeasurable.

Unfortunately, most of us seek dependence. We want companions, we want friends; we want to live in a state of separation, in a state which brings about conflict. That which is alone can never be in a state of conflict. But mind can never perceive that, can never understand that; it can only know loneliness.

Q: You said that truth can come only when one can be alone and can love sorrow. This is not clear. Kindly explain what you mean by being alone and loving sorrow.

K: Most of us are not in communion with anything. We are not directly in communion with our friends, with our wives, with our children. We are not in communion with anything directly. There are always barriers—mental, imaginary, and actual. And this separativeness is the cause, obviously, of sorrow. Don't say, 'Yes, we have read that, we know that verbally'; if you are capable of experiencing it directly, you will see that sorrow cannot come to an end by any mental process. You can explain sorrow away, which is a mental process, but sorrow is still there, though you may cover it up.

So to understand sorrow, surely you must love it. That is, you must be in direct communion with it. If you would understand something completely—your neighbour, your wife, or any relationship—you must be near it. You must come to it without any objection, prejudice, condemnation, or repulsion; you must look at it. If I would understand you, I must have no prejudices about you. I must be capable of looking at you without the barriers, screens of my prejudices and conditionings. I must be in communion with you, which means I must love you. Similarly, if I would understand sorrow, I must love it, I must be in communion with it. I cannot do so because I am running away from it through explanations, through theories, through hopes, through postponements, which are all the process of verbalization. So words prevent me from being in communion with sorrow. Words prevent me—words of explanation, rationalizations, which are still words, which are the mental process—from being directly in communion with sorrow. It is only when I am in communion with sorrow that I understand it.

The next step is: Am I, the observer of sorrow, different from sorrow? Am I, the thinker, the experiencer, different from sorrow? I have externalized it in order to do something about it, in order to avoid it, in order to conquer it, in order to run away. Am I different from that which I call sorrow? Obviously not. So I am sorrow—it is not that there is sorrow and I am different from it, I am sorrow. Then only is there a possibility of ending sorrow.

As long as I am the observer of sorrow, there is no ending of sorrow. But when there is the realization that sorrow is the 'me', that the observer himself is the sorrow, when the mind realizes it is itself sorrow—not when it is observing sorrow, not when it is feeling sorrow—that it is itself the creator of sorrow and the feeler of sorrow, then there is the ending of sorrow. This is an extraordinarily difficult thing to experience, to be aware of, because for centuries we have divided this thing. This requires, not traditional thinking, but very alert, watchful, intelligent awareness. That intelligent, integrated state is aloneness. When the observer is the observed, then it is the integrated state. And in that aloneness, in that state of being completely alone, full, when the mind is not seeking anything, not groping, neither seeking reward nor avoiding punishment, when the mind is truly still, only then does that which is not measured by the mind come into being.

Loneliness: From Commentaries on Living First Series

HER SON HAD recently died, and she said she did not know what to do now. She had so much time on her hands, she was so bored and weary and sorrowful, that she was ready to die. She had brought him up with loving care and intelligence, and he had gone to one of the best schools and to college. She had not spoiled him, though he had had everything that was necessary. She had put her faith and hope in him, and had given him all her love; for there was no one else to share it with, she and her husband having separated long ago. Her son had died through some wrong diagnosis and operation—though, she added smilingly, the doctors said that the operation was 'successful'. Now, she was left alone, and life seemed so vain and pointless. She had wept when he died, until there were no more tears, but only a dull and weary emptiness. She had had such plans for both of them, but now, she was utterly lost.

The breeze was blowing from the sea, cool and fresh, and under the tree it was quiet. The colours on the mountains were vivid, and the blue jays were very talkative. A cow wandered by, followed by her calf, and a squirrel dashed up a tree, wildly chattering. It sat on a branch and began to scold, and the scolding went on for a long time, its tail bobbing up and down. It had such sparkling bright eyes and sharp claws. A lizard came out to warm itself, and caught a fly. The tree tops were gently swaying, and a dead tree against the sky was straight and splendid. It was being bleached by the sun. There was another dead tree beside it, dark and curving, more recent in its decay. A few clouds rested on the distant mountains.

What a strange thing is loneliness, and how frightening it is! We never allow ourselves to get too close to it; and if by chance we do, we quickly run away from it. We will do anything to escape from loneliness, to cover it up. Our conscious and unconscious preoccupation seems to be to avoid it or to overcome it. Avoiding and overcoming loneliness are equally futile; though suppressed or neglected, the pain, the problem, is still there. You may lose yourself in a crowd, and yet be utterly lonely; you may be intensely active, but loneliness silently creeps upon you; put the book down, and it is there. Amusements and drinks cannot drown loneliness; you may temporarily evade it, but when the laughter and the effects of alcohol are over, the fear of loneliness returns. You may be ambitious and successful, you may have vast power over others, you may be rich in knowledge, you may worship and forget yourself in the rigmarole of rituals; but do what you will, the ache of loneliness continues. You may exist only for your son, for the Master, for the expression of your talent; but like the darkness, loneliness covers you. You may love or hate, escape from it according to your temperament and psychological demands; but loneliness is there, waiting and watching, withdrawing only to approach again.

Loneliness is the awareness of complete isolation; and are not our activities self-enclosing? Though our thoughts and emotions are expansive, are they not exclusive and dividing? Are we not seeking dominance in our relationships, in our rights and possessions, thereby creating resistance? Do we not regard work as 'yours' and 'mine'? Are we not identified with the collective, with the country, or with the few? Is not our whole tendency to isolate ourselves, to divide and separate? The very activity of the self, at whatever level, is the way of isolation; and loneliness is the consciousness of the self without activity. Activity, whether physical or psychological, becomes a means of self-expansion; and when there is no activity of any kind, there is an awareness of the emptiness of the self. It is this emptiness that we seek to fill, and in filling it we spend our life, whether at a noble or ignoble level. There may seem to be no sociological harm in filling this emptiness at a noble level; but illusion breeds untold misery and destruction, which may not be immediate. The craving to fill this emptiness—to run away from it, which is the same thing—cannot be sublimated or suppressed; for who is the entity that is to suppress or sublimate? Is not that very entity another form of craving? The objects of craving may vary, but is not all craving similar? You may change the object of your craving from drink to ideation; but without understanding the process of craving, illusion is inevitable.

There is no entity separate from craving; there is only craving, there is no one who craves. Craving takes on different masks at different times, depending on its interests. The memory of these varying interests meets the new, which brings about conflict, and so the chooser is born, establishing himself as an entity separate and distinct from craving. But the entity is not different from its qualities. The entity who tries to fill or run away from emptiness, incompleteness, loneliness, is not different from that which he is avoiding; he is it. He cannot run away from himself; all that he can do is to understand himself. He is his loneliness, his emptiness; and as long as he regards it as something separate from himself, he will be in illusion and endless conflict. When he directly experiences that he is his own loneliness, then only can there be freedom from fear. Fear exists only in relationship to an idea, and idea is the response of memory as thought. Thought is the result of experience; and though it can ponder over emptiness, have sensations with regard to it, it cannot know emptiness directly. The word *loneliness*, with its memories of pain and fear, prevents the experiencing of it afresh. The word is memory, and when the word is no longer significant, then the relationship between the experiencer and the experienced is wholly different; then that relationship is direct and not through a word, through memory; then the experiencer is the experience, which alone brings freedom from fear.

Love and emptiness cannot abide together; when there is the feeling of loneliness, love is not. You may hide emptiness under the word *love*, but when the object of your love is no longer there or does not respond, then you are aware of emptiness, you are frustrated. We use the word *love* as a means of escaping from ourselves, from our own insufficiency. We cling to the one we love, we are jealous, we miss him when he is not there and are utterly lost when he dies; and then we seek comfort in some other form, in some belief, in some substitute. Is all this love? Love is not an idea, the result of association; love is not something to be used as an escape from our own wretchedness, and when we do so use it, we make problems which have no solutions. Love is not an abstraction, but its reality can be experienced only when idea, mind, is no longer the supreme factor.

Discussion with Professor Maurice Wilkins, Brockwood Park, 12 February 1982

Maurice Wilkins[2]: It seems to me that thought is part of a creative relationship, but it is only a component in the whole thing.

Krishnamurti: Yes, but is thought love?

MW: No, it isn't, but I do wonder a little bit whether thought doesn't come into love somewhat? I mean, it is bound to, to some extent.

K: No. I wonder if love is thought.

MW: No, certainly not.

K: So is it possible to love another without thought? To love somebody means no thought; that brings about a totally different relationship, a different action.

MW: Yes, well I think there can be a great deal of thought in a loving relationship, but thought is not primary.

K: No, when there is love, thought can be used, but not the other way round.

MW: Not the other way round, yes. The basic trouble is that it tends to be the other way round. We are like computers which are being run by our programmes. For a minute I was trying to transpose what you were saying about thought coming to an end to relationship, and wondering what kind of relationship there is without thought.

K: Just see what takes place without thought. I have a relationship with my brother or my wife, and that relationship is not based on thought but basically, deeply, on love. In that love, in that strange feeling, why should I think at all? Love is comprehensive; but when thought comes into it, it is divisive, and it destroys the quality, the beauty of it.

MW: But is love comprehensive? Is it not all-pervasive rather than comprehensive, because surely love can't express itself adequately without thought?

K: Comprehensive in the sense of whole. I mean, love is not the opposite of hate.

MW: No.

K: So in itself it has no feeling of duality.

MW: I suppose love is much more a quality of the relationship, and a quality of being which pervades it.

K: Yes. When thought comes into it, then I remember all the things she did, or I did; all the troubles, the anxieties creep in. One of our great difficulties is that we really haven't understood or felt this love that is not possessiveness, attachment, jealousy, hatred, and all that.

MW: Isn't love largely awareness of the unity?

K: Would you say love has no awareness; it is love. It isn't that love is aware that we are all one. It's like a perfume. You can't dissect the perfume, or analyse the perfume. It is marvellous perfume; and the moment you analyse it, you dissipate it.

MW: Yes, if you say it is a perfume, then it is somewhat like a quality. But then quality is associated with this sense of unity, is it not?

K: But you are giving it a meaning.

MW: I am talking around it! I am not trying to pin it down. But can there be love without any awareness of this unity?

K: It is much more than that.

MW: All right, it is more than that. But can it exist if that sense of unity is not there?

K: Just a minute. Can I be a Catholic, and say I love, I have compassion? Can there be compassion, love, when there is this deep-rooted belief, idea, prejudice? Love must exist with freedom. Not the freedom to do what I like—that is nonsense; freedom of choice, and so on, has no value in what we are talking about—but there must be total freedom to love.

MW: Yes, but the Catholic might have quite a lot of love but it has limits to it in certain situations.

K: Yes, of course.

MW: But it is like asking if you can have an egg that is only partly bad! This sense of unity is part of the whole business, is it not?

K: If we have love, there is unity.

MW: Yes, all right, inevitably. I agree with you that having a sense of unity won't turn love on.

K: You see, all religions and people who are religiously minded have always attached love and devotion to a particular object, or a particular idea, a symbol; it isn't love without any hindrance to it. That's the point, sir. Can love exist when there is the self? Of course not.

MW: But if you say the self is a fixed image, then love can't exist with anything fixed because it has no limits.

K: That's right, sir.

MW: But it seems to me that in the relationship of the dialogue and movement between two minds with no sense of limit—and necessarily outside time, because time would be putting a limit—then something new can come up.

K: Ah, but can two minds ever meet? Are they like two parallel railway lines that never meet? Is our relationship with each other as human beings, wife and husband, and so on, always parallel, each pursuing his own line, and never actually meeting in the sense of having real love for another, or even of love without an object?

MW: Well, in practice there always is some degree of separation.

K: Yes, that's all I am saying.

MW: If the relationship can be on a different level, then there are no longer lines separated in space.

K: Of course, but to come to that level seems almost impossible. I am attached to my wife, I tell her I love her, and she is attached to me. Is that love? I possess her, she possesses me, or she likes being possessed, and so on, all the complications of relationship. But I say to her, or she says to me, 'I love you', and that seems to satisfy us. I question whether that is love at all.

MW: Well, it makes people feel more comfortable for a time.

K: And is comfort love?

MW: It is limited, and when one partner dies, the other is miserable.

K: Yes, with loneliness, tears, suffering. We really should discuss this thing. I used to know a man to whom money was God. He had plenty of money, and when he was dying, he wanted to look at all the things he possessed. The possessions were him; he was dying to the possessions outwardly, but the outward possessions were himself. And he was frightened, not of this state of coming to an end, but of losing that. Do you understand? Losing that, not losing himself and finding something new.

MW: Could I just ask a question about death? What about a man who is dying and wants to see all the people he has known, all his friends, before he dies; is that an attachment to these relationships?

K: Yes, that is attachment. He is going to die and death is rather lonely, it is a most exclusive club, exclusive action. In that state I want to meet my wife, children, grandchildren, because I know I am going to lose them all; I am going to die, end. It's a terrifying thing. The other day I saw a man who was dying. Sir, I have never seen such fear, such absolute fear of ending. He said, 'I am frightened of separation from my family, from the money I have had, from the things I have done. This is my family. I love them, and I'm scared stiff of losing them'.

MW: But I suppose the man might want to see all his friends and his family to say . . .

K: 'Goodbye, old boy, we will meet on the other side'! That's another matter.

MW: Possibly.

K: I knew a man, sir, who told his family, 'Next year, in January, I am going to die on such and such a date'. And on that date he invited all his friends and his family. He said, 'I am dying today', and made the will. 'Please leave me'. They all trooped out of the room, and he died!

MW: Yes, well, if the relationships with all these other people were important to him and he was going to die, he would just like to see them the last time, and now it is finished. 'I am finished, I die'. That was not an attachment.

K: No, of course not. The consequence of attachment is painful, anxious; there is a certain sense of agony, of losing.

MW: Constant insecurity, fear.

K: Insecurity, and all the rest, follows. And that I call love. I say I love my wife, and deep inside I know all the travail of this attachment, but I can't let go.

MW: But you still feel distressed that your wife would be sad when you die.

K: Oh yes, that is part of the game, part of the whole business. She soon gets over it and marries somebody else, and carries on the game.

MW: Yes, one would hope so, but one could be worried and afraid of other people's sorrow.

K: Yes, sir.

MW: Presumably the acceptance of one's own death would reduce their sorrow.

K: No. Is sorrow attached to fear? I am afraid of death; I am afraid of ending my career; all the things I have accumulated both physically and inwardly come to an end. Fear then invents reincarnation and all that business. Can I really be free from the fear of death? Which means: Can I live with death? Not that I commit suicide; I live with it, thrilled with the ending of things, the ending of my attachment. Would my wife tolerate it if I said, 'I have ended my attachment to you'? There would be agony. I am questioning this whole content of consciousness put there by thought. Thought dominates our lives, and I ask myself if thought can have its own place, and only that place, and interfere nowhere else. Why should I have thought in my relationship with my friend, or with my wife, or my girl? Why should I think about it? When somebody says, 'I am thinking of you', it sounds so silly.

MW: Well, one often does need to think of other people for practical reasons, of course.

K: That's a different matter. But I am saying, where love is, why should thought exist? Thought in relationship is destructive. It is attachment, it is possession, it is clinging to each other for comfort, for safety, for security; and all that is not love.

MW: No, but as you said, love can make use of thought, and there is what you call a thoughtfulness in relationship.

K: That's a different matter, yes. Look, if I am attached to my wife, or my husband, or to a piece of furniture, I love in that attachment, and the consequences of that are incalculably harmful. Can I love my wife without attachment? How marvellous it is to love somebody wanting nothing from them.

MW: That's a great freedom.

K: Yes, sir. So love is freedom.

MW: But you appear to imply that if there is love between husband and wife and one dies, the other would not have sorrow. I think maybe that's right.

K: I think so. That's right, sir.

MW: You would transcend sorrow.

K: Sorrow is thought, sorrow is an emotion, sorrow is a shock, sorrow is a sense of loss, the feeling of losing somebody and suddenly finding yourself utterly desolated and lonely.

MW: Yes. You mean a state of loneliness is contrary to nature, so to speak.

K: So if I could understand the nature of ending—ending something all the time: ending my ambition, ending sorrow, ending fear, ending the complexity of desire. To end it; which is death. It is necessary to die every day to everything that you have gathered psychologically.

MW: And everyone agrees that death is freedom.

K: That is real freedom.

MW: There is no difficulty in appreciating that. You mean you want to transpose that ultimate freedom into all one's life.

K: Yes, sir. Otherwise we are slaves, slaves to choice, slaves to everything.

MW: Not masters of time, but slaves of time.

K: Slaves of time, yes.

2. Professor Maurice Wilkins of the University of London. He is a Nobel Prize winner in biology.

New York, 24 April 1971: From The Awakening of Intelligence

WE MUST LOOK at our relationship as it actually is now, every day; and in observing what it is, we shall discover how to bring about a change in that actuality. So we are describing what actually is. Each one lives in his own world, in his world of ambition, greed, fear, the desire to succeed, and so on. If I am married, I have responsibilities, children; I go to the office or some place of work; husband and wife, boy and girl, meet each other in bed. And that's what we call love—leading separate lives, being isolated, building a wall of resistance around ourselves, pursuing a self-centred activity. Each one is seeking security psychologically; each one is depending on the other for comfort, for pleasure, for companionship. Because each one is so deeply lonely, each demands to be loved, to be cherished, each one is trying to dominate the other. You can see this for yourself if you observe yourself. Is there any kind of relationship at all? There is no relationship between two human beings; though they may have children, a house, actually, they are not related. If they have a common project, that project sustains them, holds them together, but that's not relationship.

Realizing all this, one sees that if there is no relationship between two human beings, then corruption begins, not in the outward structure of society, in the outer phenomenon of pollution, but in the inner pollution, destruction. Human beings actually have no relationship at all—as you haven't. You may hold the hand of another, kiss each other, sleep together, but actually, when you observe very closely, is there any relationship at all? To be related means not to be dependent on each other, not to escape from your loneliness through another, not to try to find comfort, companionship, through another. When you seek comfort through another, are dependent, and so on, can there be any kind of relationship? Aren't you then using each other?

We are not being cynical, but actually observing what is; that is not cynicism. To find out what it actually means to be related to another, one must understand this question of loneliness, because most of us are terribly lonely; the older we grow, the more lonely we become, especially in this country. Have you noticed what old people are like? Have you noticed their escapes, their amusements? They have worked all their lives, and they want to escape into some kind of entertainment.

Seeing this, can we find a way of living in which we don't use another, psychologically, emotionally, not depend on another, not use another as a means of escape from our own tortures, from our own despairs, from our own loneliness?

To understand this is to understand what it means to be lonely. Have you ever been lonely? Do you know what it means? That you have no relationship with another, are completely isolated. You may be with your family, in a crowd, in the office, wherever you are, when this complete sense of utter loneliness with its despair suddenly comes upon you. Until you solve that completely, your relationship becomes a means of escape and therefore it leads to corruption, to misery. How is one to understand this loneliness, this sense of complete isolation? To understand it, one has to look at one's own life. Is not your every action a self-centred activity? You may occasionally be charitable, generous, do something without any motive—those are rare occasions. This despair can never be dissolved through escape, but only by observing it.

So we have come back to this question of how to observe ourselves so that in that observation there is no conflict at all. Because conflict is corruption, is waste of energy; it is the battle of our life, from the moment we are born till we die. Is it possible to live without a single moment of conflict? To do that, to find that out for ourselves, we have to learn how to observe our whole movement. There is observation that is true when the observer is not and there is only observation.

When there is no relationship, can there be love? We talk about it, and love, as we know it, is related to sex and pleasure, isn't it? Some of you say 'No'. When you say no, then you must be without ambition, then there must be no competition, no division—as 'you' and 'me', 'we' and 'they'. There must be no division of nationality, or the division brought about by belief, by knowledge. Then only can you say you love. But for most people love is related to sex and pleasure and all the travail that comes with it—jealousy, envy, antagonism—you know what happens between man and woman. When that relationship is not true, real, deep, completely harmonious, then how can you have peace in the world? How can there be an end to war?

So relationship is one of the most—or rather the most—important thing in life. That means that one has to understand what love is. Surely, one comes upon it strangely, without asking for it. When you find out for yourself what love is not, then you know what love is. Not theoretically, not verbally, but when you realize actually what it is not: not to have a mind that is competitive, ambitious, a mind that is striving, comparing, imitating. Such a mind cannot possibly love.

So can you, living in this world, live completely without ambition, completely without ever comparing yourself with another? Because the moment you compare, then there is conflict, there is envy, there is the desire to achieve, to go beyond the other.

Can a mind and a heart that remembers the hurts, the insults, the things that have made it insensitive and dull—can such a mind and heart know what love is? Is love pleasure? And yet that is what we are pursuing, consciously or unconsciously. Our gods are the result of our pleasure. Our beliefs, our social structure, the morality of society—which is essentially immoral—is the result of our pursuit of pleasure. And when you say, 'I love somebody', is it love? That means no separation, no domination, no self-centred activity. To find out what it is, one must deny all this—deny it in the sense of seeing the falseness of it. When you once see something as false—which you have accepted as true, as natural, as human—then you can never go back to it; when you see a dangerous snake, or a dangerous animal, you never play with it, you never come near it. Similarly, when you actually see that love is none of these things, feel it, observe it, chew it, live with it, are totally committed to it, then you will know what love is, what compassion is—which means passion for everyone.

We have no passion; we have lust, we have pleasure. The root meaning of the word passion is sorrow. We have all had sorrow of some kind or another, losing somebody, the sorrow of self-pity, the sorrow of the human race, both collective and personal. We know what sorrow is, the death of someone whom you consider you have loved. When we remain with that sorrow totally, without trying to rationalize it, without trying to escape from it in any form—through words or through action—when you remain with it completely, without any movement of thought, then you will find that out of that sorrow comes passion. That passion has the quality of love, and love has no sorrow.

❖

CAN YOU FIND out how to live a life now, today, in which there is always an ending to everything that you began? Not in your office, of course, but inwardly, to end all the knowledge that you have gathered—knowledge being your experiences, your memories, your hurts, the comparative way of living, comparing yourself always with somebody else. To end all that every day, so that the next day your mind is fresh and young. Such a mind can never be hurt, and that is innocence.

One has to find out for oneself what it means to die; then there is no fear, therefore every day is a new day—and I really mean this, one can do this—so that your mind and your eyes see life as something totally new. That is eternity. That is the quality of the mind that has come upon this timeless state, because it has known what it means to die every day to everything it has collected during the day. Surely, in that there is love. Love is something totally new every day, but pleasure is not, pleasure has continuity. Love is always new, and therefore it is its own eternity.

Do you want to ask any questions?

Questioner: You seem to believe in sharing, but at the same time you say that two lovers, or husband and wife, cannot base their love, shouldn't base their love, on comforting each other. I don't see anything wrong in comforting each other; that is sharing.

Krishnamurti: What do you share? What are we sharing now? We talked about death, we talked about love, about the necessity of total revolution, about complete psychological change, not to live in the old pattern of formulas, of struggle, pain, imitation, conformity, and all the rest of those things man has lived through millennia and produced this marvellous, messy world! We have talked about death. How do we share that together? Share the understanding of it, not the verbal statement, not the description, not the explanations of it? What does it mean to share the understanding, to share the truth which comes with the understanding? And what does understanding mean? You tell me something which is serious, which is vital, which is relevant, important, and I listen to it completely, because it is vital to me. To listen vitally, my mind must be quiet, mustn't it? If I am chattering, if I am looking somewhere else, if I am comparing what you are saying with what I know, my mind is not quiet. It is only when my mind is quiet and listens completely that there is understanding of the truth of the thing. We share that together; otherwise we can't share. We can't share the words, we can only share the truth of something. You and I can only see the truth of something when the mind is totally committed to the observation.

You see the beauty of a sunset, the lovely hills, the shadows and the moonlight. How do you share it with a friend? By telling him, 'Do look at that marvellous hill'? You may say it, but is that sharing? When you actually share something with another, it means you must both have the same intensity, at the same time, at the same level. Otherwise you can't share, can you? You must both have a common interest, at the same level, with the same passion; otherwise how can you share something? You can share a piece of bread, but that's not what we are talking about.

To see together, which is sharing together, both of us must see—not agree or disagree—but see together what actually is; not interpret it according to my conditioning or your conditioning, but see together what it is. And to see together one must be free to observe, one must be free to listen. That means to have no prejudice. Then only, with that quality of love, is there sharing.

Q: Sir, when you speak of relationships, you speak always of a man and a woman or a girl and a boy. Will the same things you say about relationships also apply to a man and a man, or a woman and a woman?

K: Homosexuality?

Q: If you wish to give it that name, sir, yes.

K: You see, when we are talking of love, whether it is of man and man, woman and woman, or man and woman, we are not talking of a particular kind of relationship, we are talking about the whole movement, the whole sense of relationship, not a relationship with one or two. Don't you know what it means to be related to the world, when you feel you are the world? Not as an idea—that's appalling—but actually to feel that you are responsible, that you are committed to this responsibility. That is the only commitment; not to be committed through bombs, or committed to a particular activity, but to feel that you are the world and the world is you. Unless you change completely, radically, and bring about a total mutation in yourself, do what you will outwardly but there will be no peace for man. If you feel that in your blood, then your questions will be related entirely to the present and to bringing about a change in the present, not to some speculative ideals.

Brockwood Park, 30 August 1977

Krishnamurti: With all your experiences, with all your knowledge, with all the civilization that you have behind you of which you are the result, why is there no compassion in your daily life? To find out why you don't have it, why it doesn't exist in the human heart and mind and outlook, don't you ask also the question: Do you love anybody?

Questioner: I wonder, sir, what love is all about.

K: Please, sir, I am asking you most respectfully whether you love anybody at all? You may love your dog, but the dog is your slave. Apart from animals and buildings and books and poetry and the love of the land, do you love anybody? That means not asking anything in return, not asking anything from that person you love, not being dependent on that person at all. Because if you are dependent, then fear, jealousy, anxiety, hatred, anger begin. If you are attached to somebody, is that love? Find out! And if all that is not love—I am just asking, I don't say it is or it is not—then how can you have compassion? We are asking for something much more than love when we don't even have just ordinary love for another human being.

Q: How do you find that love?

K: I don't want to find that love. All I want to do is to remove that which is not love, to be free of jealousy, attachment.

Q: That means we should have no fragmentation.

K: Sir, that is just theory. Find out if you love somebody. How can you love when you are concerned about yourself, your problems, your ambitions, your desire for success, your desire for so much, putting yourself first and the other second? Or the other first and you second, it is the same thing.

We have asked so many questions. Can we sit together and go into whether I can be free of attachment, understanding even verbally that love cannot exist when there is jealousy or attachment? I will have a dialogue with myself, shall I, and you listen?

I realize by listening to this that I don't love. That is a fact. I am not going to deceive myself. I am not going to pretend to my wife that I love her—or to a woman or a girl or boy. Now, first of all, I don't know what love is. But I do know that I am jealous; I do know that I am terribly attached to someone, and that in that attachment there is fear, there is jealousy, there is anxiety, there is a sense of dependency. I don't like to depend, but I depend because I am lonely and I'm shoved around by society, in the office, in the factory, and I come home and I want to feel comfort, companionship, to escape from myself. So I am dependent, attached to that person. Now, I am asking myself how I am to be free of this attachment, not knowing what love is. I won't pretend I have love of God, love of Jesus, love of Krishna; I throw out all that nonsense. How am I to be free of this attachment? I am taking that just as an example.

I won't run away from it. Right? I don't know how it is going to end up with my wife; when I am really detached from her, my relationship to her may change. She might be attached to me and I might not be attached to her or to any other woman. You understand? It isn't that I want to be detached from her and join another woman; that is silly. So what shall I do? I won't run away from the consequence of being totally free of all attachment. I am going to investigate. I don't know what love is, but I see very clearly, definitely, without any doubt, that attachment to a person means fear, anxiety, jealousy, possession, and so on. So I ask myself how I am to be free of attachment? Not a method. I want freedom from it, but I really don't know how. I am having a dialogue with myself.

So I begin to inquire. Then I get caught in a system. I get caught up with some guru who says, 'I will help you to be detached; do this and this, practise this and this'. I want to be free from it, and I accept what the silly man says because I see the importance of being free, and he promises me that if I do this I will have a reward. So I want to be free in order to have a reward. You understand? I am looking for a reward. So I see how silly I am: I want to be free and I get attached to the reward.

I represent the rest of humanity—and I really mean it—therefore if I am having a dialogue with myself, I am in tears. It is a passion for me.

I don't want to be attached, and yet I find myself getting attached to an idea. That is, I must be free, and someone's book or idea says, 'Do this and you will have that'. So the reward becomes my attachment. Then I say, 'Look what I have done. Be careful, don't get caught in that trap. Whether it is a woman or an idea, it is still attachment'. I have learned that exchanging it for something else is still attachment. So I am very watchful now. Then I say to myself, 'Is there a way, or what am I to do, to be free of attachment? What is my motive? Why do I want to be free from attachment? Because it is painful? Because I want to achieve a state where there is no attachment, no fear, and so on?' Please follow me because I am representing you. What is my motive in wanting to be free? I suddenly realize a motive gives a direction, and that direction will dictate my freedom. Why do I have a motive? What is motive? A motive is a movement, a hope to achieve something. So the motive is my attachment. The motive has become my attachment, not only the woman, the idea of a goal, but my motive; I must have that. So I am always functioning within the field of attachment. I am attached to the woman, the future, and the motive. So I say,

'Oh, my God, it is a tremendously complex thing. I didn't realize that to be free of attachment implies all this'.

Now, I see this as clearly as I see a map: the villages, the side roads, the main roads. Then I say to myself, 'Is it possible for me to be free of my motive, to which I am attached, to be free of the woman for whom I have great attachment, and also be free of the reward that I think I am going to get when I am free? Why am I attached to all this? Is it that I am insufficient in myself? Is it that I am very, very lonely and I want to escape from that extraordinary sense of isolation and therefore cling to something—a man, a woman, an idea, a motive? Is it that I am lonely and that I am escaping from that feeling of extraordinary isolation through attachment to another?'

So I am not interested in attachment at all. I am interested in understanding why I am lonely, which makes me attached. I am lonely, and that loneliness has forced me to escape through attachment to something or someone. As long as I am lonely, the whole sequence is this. So I must investigate why I am lonely. What does it mean to be lonely? How does it come about? Is loneliness instinctual, inbred, hereditary, or is it my daily activity that is bringing this about?

I question because I accept nothing. I don't accept that it is instinct and say that I can't help it. I don't accept that it is heredity and that therefore I am not to blame. As I don't accept any of these things, I ask, 'Why is there this loneliness?' I question it and remain with the question, not try to find an answer. I have asked myself what is the root of this loneliness; and I am watching, I am not trying to find an intellectual answer; I am not trying to tell the loneliness what it should do, or what it is. I am watching it for it to tell me.

There is a watchfulness for the loneliness to reveal itself. It won't reveal itself if I run away, if I am frightened, if I resist it. So I watch it. I watch it so that no thought interferes, because this is much more important than thought coming in. My whole energy is concerned with the observation of that loneliness; therefore thought doesn't come in at all. The mind is being challenged and it must answer. When you are challenged, it is a crisis. In a crisis you have all the energy, and that energy remains if it is not interfered with. This is a challenge which must be answered.

Q: How can we hang on to that energy? How can we do something about this energy?

K: It has come. You have lost the whole thing.

Look, I started out having a dialogue with myself. I asked, 'What is this strange thing called love?' Everybody talks about it, writes about it; there are romantic poems, pictures and all the rest of it, sex and the whole mess of it. And I ask if I have this thing called love, if there is such a thing as love. I see that love doesn't exist when there is jealousy, hatred, fear. So I am not concerned with love any more; I am concerned with 'what is', that is, my fear, attachment, and why I am attached. I say maybe one of the reasons, not the whole reason, is that I am lonely, desperately isolated. The older I grow, the more I am in isolation. So I watch it. It is a challenge to find out, and because it is a challenge all energy is there to respond. That is simple, isn't it? When there is death in the family, it is a challenge. If there is some catastrophe, an accident, it is a challenge and you have the energy to meet it. You don't say, 'Where do you get this energy?' When your house is on fire, you have the energy to move. You have extraordinary energy. You don't sit back and say, 'Well, I must get this energy', and then wait. Then the whole house would be burned.

So there is tremendous energy to answer the question why there is this loneliness. I have rejected ideas, suppositions, or theories of heredity or instinct. All that means nothing to me. It is 'what is'. So why am I lonely—not I—why is there this loneliness which every human being, if he is at all aware, goes through, superficially or most profoundly? Why does this come into being? Does the mind do something that brings it? You understand? Having rejected theories, instincts, heredity, I am asking if the mind brings this about.

Is the mind doing this? Loneliness means total isolation. Is the mind, the brain, doing this? The mind is partly the movement of thought. Is thought doing this? Is thought in daily life creating, bringing about this sense of isolation? Am I isolating myself because I want to become bigger in the office, become the executive—or the bishop, or the pope? It is working all the time isolating itself. Are you watching this?

Q: I think it isolates itself in relation to how crowded it is.

K: Yes.

Q: As a reaction.

K: Yes, that is right, sir, that is right. I want to go into this. I see that thought, the mind, is all the time operating to make itself superior, greater, working itself towards this isolation.

The problem then is: Why does thought do this? Is it the nature of thought to work for itself? Is it the nature of thought to create this isolation? Does society create this isolation? Does education create this isolation? Education does bring about this isolation; it prepares us for a certain specialized career. I have found that thought is the response of the past as knowledge, experience, and memory, so I know that thought is limited, that thought is timebinding. So thought is doing this. So my concern then is why thought does it. Is it in its very nature to do this?

❖

Q: What is really inside is being hidden all the time, and therefore thought must be deceptive, must lead to isolation, because nobody knows what anybody else is feeling because of all the pretence.

K: We have been through that, sir. We are coming to the point when we are not pretending.

We said in the dialogue that we don't know what love is. I know when we use that word *love* there is a certain pretence, a certain hypocrisy, putting on a certain type of mask. We have been through all that. We have come to the point now of asking why thought, being a fragment, brings about this isolation—if it does. I have found it does in my conversation with myself because I have seen that thought is limited, that thought is time-binding, that whatever it does must be limited, and that in that limitation it has found security. It has found security in saying, 'I have a special career in life'. It has found security in saying, 'I am a professor and so I am perfectly safe'. And you are stuck there for the rest of your life. In that there is great psychological security as well as factual security.

So thought is doing this. The problem then is: Can thought realize that it is limited, and that therefore whatever it does is limited and therefore fragmentary and therefore isolating? Whatever it does will be this? This is a very important point: Can thought realize its own limitations, or does thought say to itself, 'I am limited'? You understand the difference? Thought being me, do I say that thought is limited, or does thought itself realize I am limited? The two things are entirely different. One is an imposition, and therefore conflict; whereas when thought itself says, 'I am limited', it won't move away from that limitation. This is very important to understand because it is the real essence of the thing. We are imposing on thought what it should do. Thought has created the 'me', and the 'me' has separated itself from thought and says it will tell thought what it should do. But if thought realizes itself that it is limited, then there is no resistance, no conflict, it says, 'I am that. I am through'.

In my dialogue with myself, I am asking if thought realizes this itself, or am I telling it that it is limited. If I am telling it that it is limited, then I become separate from the limitations. Then I struggle to overcome the limitations; therefore there is conflict, which is violence, which is not love. So does thought realize itself that it is limited? I have to find out. I am being challenged. I have energy now because I am challenged.

Put it differently. Does consciousness realize its content? **Does consciousness realize its content is itself?** Have I heard another say, 'Consciousness is its content, its content makes up consciousness', and therefore I say, 'Yes it is so'; or does consciousness—my consciousness, this consciousness—realize its content and therefore that its very content is the totality of my consciousness? Do you see the difference in the two? One is imposed by me, the 'me' created by thought, and if 'I' impose something on thought, then there is conflict. It is like a tyrannical government imposing itself—but I have created this government.

We are asking if thought has realized its own littleness, its own pettiness, its own limitations? Or is it pretending to be something extraordinary, noble, divine? That is nonsense, because thought is memory, experience. In my dialogue there must be clarity about this point: there is no outside influence imposing on thought that it is limited. Because there is no imposition, there is no conflict, therefore it realizes it is limited. It sees that whatever it does, even its worship of God, is limited, shoddy, petty—though it has created marvellous cathedrals throughout Europe.

In my conversation with myself, there has been a discovery that loneliness is created by thought. And thought has now realized itself that it is limited and that it cannot solve the problem of loneliness. As it cannot solve the problem of loneliness, does loneliness exist? Thought has made this sense of loneliness. Thought realizes that it is limited, and that because it is limited, fragmentary, divided, it has created this emptiness, loneliness. Therefore when it realizes this, loneliness is not.

Then there is freedom from attachment. I have done nothing but watch attachment and what is implied in attachment—greed, fear, loneliness—and by tracing it, looking at it, observing it—not analysing it, examining it, but just looking, looking, looking—there is a discovery that thought has done all this. Thought, because it is fragmentary, has created this attachment. When it realizes this, attachment ceases. There is no effort made at all, because the moment there is effort it is back again.

We have said that if there is love, there is no attachment, and if there is attachment, there is no love. So there has been the **removal of the major factor through negation of what it is not.** Do you know what it means in your daily life: no remembrance of anything my wife, my girlfriend, or my neighbour told me; no remembrance of any hurt; no attachment to the image about her. I was attached to the image thought had created about her—that she has hurt me, she has bullied me, she has given me comfort sexually, ten different things; all are the movement of thought which has created the image, and it is the image I was attached to. So attachment has gone.

There are other factors: fear, pleasure, comfort in that person, or in that idea. Now, must I get through all these step by step, one by one, or are they all over? Must I investigate fear and the desire for comfort as I have investigated attachment? Must I observe why I seek comfort? Is it because I am insufficient that I want comfort, that I want a comfortable chair, a comfortable woman or man, or a comfortable idea? I think most of us do want to have a comfortable, secure idea which can never be shaken. I get terribly attached to it, and if anybody says it is nonsense, I get angry, I get jealous, I get upset because he is shaking my house. I see I don't have to go through the investigation of all those various factors. If I see it at one glance, I have captured it.

So through negation of what is not love, the other thing is. I don't have to ask what love is. I don't have to run after it. If I run after it, it is not love, it is a reward. In my inquiry, slowly, carefully, without distortion, without illusion, I have negated everything that it is not, and the other is.

Saanen, 18 July 1978

P<small>LEASE, WE ARE</small> going into something which is perhaps rather difficult. I don't know where it is going to lead us. It may become a little more complex, so please give a little attention.

You know, when you have a small child with you, you listen to its cries, you listen to its words, its murmurs. You are so concerned you listen; you may be asleep, but the moment he cries you wake up. You are attentive all the time because the child is yours, you must care for it, you must love it, you must hold it. You are so tremendously attentive that even though you are asleep, you wake up. Now, with that same quality of attention, affection, care, you give to every movement of that child, could you watch the mirror which is yourself? Not me, you are not listening to me; you are listening with that extraordinary concentrated affection and care to the mirror which is yourself, and to what it is telling you. Will you do it?

We are asking why human beings have become so mechanical. Mechanical habit obviously produces disorder because energy functioning always within a narrow limit is struggling to break through, which is the essence of conflict. Do you understand what the mirror is saying?—not me, there is no speaker here. Can you observe with care, with attention, with a feeling of great affection, what you are listening to?

We are talking about disorder. We live in a disorder of habits, of beliefs, of conclusions, of opinions. This is the pattern we live in, which naturally, being limited, must create disorder. Now, when one is in disorder, to seek order is wrong, because the mind that is confused, unclear, in seeking what is order will also be confused, will also be uncertain. That is clear. But whereas, if you look into disorder, if you understand the disorder in which you live and the causes of the movement of disorder, in the very understanding of it, order naturally comes—easily, happily, without any compulsion, without any control. The mirror is telling you that you can discover the causes instantly—not verbally, intellectually, or emotionally—of this movement of disorder in oneself and why it comes about, if you give attention, the same attention that you give to a small, defenceless child. That is having an insight into disorder.

What is the root of disorder? There are many causes of disorder: comparison, comparing oneself with another, comparing oneself with what one 'should be', imitating an example, some saint; conforming, adjusting to something you think is beyond that which is. There is always conflict between 'what is' and 'what should be'. To compare is the movement of thought: I was this, or I was happy and some day I will be happy again. This constant measurement between 'what has been' or 'what is' and 'what should be', this constant evaluation brings conflict. That is one of the basic reasons of disorder.

Another cause of disorder is operating from the past. Now, is love a movement of time, of thought, of remembrance? Do you understand the question the mirror in which you are looking is asking you? Doesn't what we call *love* create extraordinary disorder in human relationships? Look at it yourself.

What is the root of disorder? You can see the causes and we can add more; that is irrelevant. In examining what is the root of it, don't analyse. Just look. If you look without analysis, you have an immediate insight into it. If you say, 'I will examine, I will deduce', or analyse it from outside through induction and deduction, it is still the movement of thought. Whereas if you can observe with care, with deep attention in which is involved a great deal of tenderness, affection, then you have an insight. Go on, find out.

What is the root of our disorder—inward disorder and therefore outward disorder? You can see what terrible disorder there is in the world, agonizing disorder; people are killing each other, dissidents are being put into prison and tortured. We tolerate all that because our minds accept things, or try to change a little bit here and there. To see the root of disorder, you have to go into the question: What is our consciousness? As you look at yourself in that undistorted mirror, what is your consciousness? That may be the essence of disorder. We have to investigate together what our consciousness is.

Our consciousness is a living thing, a moving thing; it is active, not something static, closed, locked up. It is something that is constantly changing, but changing within a small, limited border. It is like a man thinking he is changing when he changes a little bit in one corner and doesn't transform the rest of the field. We have to understand the nature and the structure of consciousness. We are doing that to find out if that is the root of our disorder. It may not be. We are going to find out. What is our consciousness? Is it not everything that thought has put together: the form, the body, the name, the senses with which thought has identified itself, the beliefs, the pains, the tortures, the agonies, the discomforts, the depressions and elations, the jealousies, the anxieties, the fears, the pleasures, my country and your country, belief in God and no belief in God, saying Jesus is the most important, Krishna is much more important, and so on, and so on, and so on. Is not all that your consciousness? You can add more to it: I am brown, I wish I were lighter; I am black but black is beautiful, and so on, and so on. The past, heredity, mythology, the whole tradition of mankind, is based essentially on this. All that is the content, and as long as one is unaware of the content of consciousness and acts, then that action must be limited and therefore create disorder. Thought in its movement must create disorder unless thought has realized its proper place. Knowledge is limited and therefore it has its proper place. That is clear.

Thought born of yesterday, or ten thousand million yesterdays, is limited, and the content of our consciousness is therefore limited. In whatever way thought may say that this consciousness isn't limited, or that there is a higher consciousness, it is still a form of consciousness. So thought which hasn't realized its proper place is the very essence of disorder. This is not something romantic, vague, nonsensical; you can see for yourself, if you are logical, sane, clear, that thought, being limited, must create disorder. A man who says, 'I am a Jew', or 'I am an Arab', is limited and therefore closing himself, resisting; therefore wars and all the misery begin. Do you actually see this fact, not as an idea, not as something that somebody is telling you, but see it for yourself, as you hear the cry of the baby? Then you act. You get up.

Part of our mechanical way of living is born out of this limited consciousness. Is it possible not to expand consciousness, not enlarge it, not add more things to it, more knowledge, more experience, more moving from one corner to another? There are schools which are trying to expand consciousness, by practice, by discipline, control. When you are trying to expand consciousness, there is a centre of measurement. When you try to enlarge anything—enlarge a house from a small foundation to a larger foundation—there is a centre from which you enlarge. Similarly, there is a centre from which there is an expanding, which is measuring. Look at yourself. Aren't you trying to expand your consciousness? You may not use that word. You may say, 'Well, I am trying to be better', 'I am trying to be more this or that, or to achieve'. As long as there is a centre from which you act, there must be disorder.

Then the problem arises: Is it possible to act, function naturally, happily without a centre, without the content of consciousness? We are putting fundamental questions. You may not be used to that. Most of us put questions rather slackly, or indifferently, and move off. But we are asking questions that you must answer, must go into to discover the answers for yourself. Is it possible to act, to live our daily life, without the centre? The centre is the essence of disorder. In your relationship with another, however intimate it may be, if you are always concerned about yourself, your ambitions, your personality, your beauty, your habits, and the other is also doing the same, naturally there is conflict, which is disorder.

Is it possible not to act from the centre, which is this consciousness with its content, all the things which thought has put together, with its sensations, with its desires, with its fears, and so on? What is the action in which there is no contradiction, no regret, no reward or punishment, and which is therefore an action that is whole? We are going to find out. It is not that I am going to find out and tell you, but together we are going to find out, remembering that there is no speaker but only the mirror in which you are looking. To understand it we must go into the question of what love is. Because if we can find the truth of what love is, that may completely dissolve the centre, completely bring about a holistic action. So we must go into it very, very carefully—if you are willing to listen. You have your opinions about love. You have your conclusions about love. You say love cannot exist without jealousy, love exists only when there is sex, love exists only when you love all your neighbours, love animals. You have a concept, an idea, a conclusion about what love is. If you have this then you cannot possibly investigate. If you already say, 'This is so', you are finished. It is like one of those gurus who says, 'I know, I have reached enlightenment', and you, being gullible, follow him. You never question him.

Here there is no authority, there is no speaker, but we are asking a very, very serious question that may resolve the conflict, the constant battle between oneself and another. To find that out, we must go very deeply into this question of what love is. We are just talking of what human beings call *love:* love for their animals, their pets, love for their garden, love for their house, love for their furniture, love for their girl or boy, love for their gods, love for their country—this thing called *love*, which is so loaded, which is so trodden upon. We are going to find out what it is.

The baby is crying, so please pay a little attention. You know when the baby cries, you are listening with all your mind. There is an art of listening. The word *art* implies putting everything in its right place. If you understand the meaning of that word, the real art is not painting pictures, but the art of putting your life in its proper place, which is to live harmoniously. When you have put everything in yourself in its right place, you are free. Putting everything in its right place is part of intelligence. You will say we are giving a new meaning to that word *intelligence*. One must. Intelligence implies reading between the lines, between the words, between two silences, between speech, listening with your mind all the time alert to listen. You hear not only with the ear, but also without the ear.

We are asking: What is the meaning and the beauty—if there is beauty—of love? Have you ever considered what beauty is? What does beauty mean? Is it connected to desire? Don't deny it, look at it, listen carefully and find out. Is beauty part of desire? Is beauty part of the senses? You see a marvellous building, the Parthenon, or one of the cathedrals, marvellous buildings; your senses are awakened by the beauty of that. So is beauty part of this? Is beauty in the colour, the shape, the bones of the face, the clarity in the eyes, and the skin and the hair, in the expression of a man or a woman? Or is there another quality of beauty which may transcend all this beauty; and when that is part of this life, then the form, the face, everything has its place? If that is not captured, if that is not understood, the outward expression becomes all important. We are going to find out what that beauty is if you are interested.

You know when you see something like a marvellous mountain against the blue sky, the vivid, bright, clear, unpolluted snow, the majesty of it drives all your thoughts, your concerns, your problems away. Have you noticed that? You say, 'How beautiful it is', and for two seconds perhaps, or for even a minute, you are absolutely silent. The grandeur of it drives away for that second the pettiness of ourselves. So that immensity has taken us over. Like a child occupied with an intricate toy for an hour; he won't talk, he won't make any noise, he is completely absorbed in that. The toy has absorbed him. So the mountain absorbs you and therefore for the second, or the minute, you are absolutely quiet, which means there is no self. Now, without being absorbed by something—either a toy, a mountain, a face, or an idea—to be completely without the me in oneself, is the essence of beauty.

We are going to find what love is. If we can, our life may be totally different; one may live without conflict, without control, without any form of effort. We are going to find out.

Besides positive action, there is an action which is non-action. Action which is considered positive is doing something about something, controlling, suppressing, making effort, dominating, avoiding, explaining, rationalizing, analysing. We are saying there is non-action, which is not related to positive action, is not the opposite of it, which is to observe without action. Then that very observation brings about a radical transformation in that which is being observed, which is non-action. We are so used to acting positively: 'I must', 'I must not', 'This is right', 'This is wrong', 'This is correct', 'This should be', 'This must not be', 'I'll suppress it', 'I'll control'. All this is struggling with the 'me', which is the essence of disorder, which is the essence of conflict. If you see that, not verbally or intellectually, or optically, but actually see the truth of it, then there is non-action, in which there is no effort. Mere observation itself changes that which is being observed.

We are asking: What is love? We said that we have many opinions about it, opinions of specialists, opinions of gurus, opinions of priests; your wife says or your girl says, 'This is love', or you say, 'That is love', or you say it is related to sex, and so on. Is it? Is it related to the senses? From the senses arises desire. The movement of the senses is desire, obviously. I see a beautiful thing, the senses are awakened, and I want it. Look at it for yourself. We are saying that when there is the total movement of the senses—all the senses, not a particular sense—then desire is non-existent. You think it out.

Is love the movement of the senses with desire? To put it differently, is love desire? The senses are in operation sexually all the time: the remembrance, the pictures, the images, the sensations. The movement of all that is considered love. Love, as far as one can observe, is part of desire. Go slowly. We are going into it. Is love attachment? I am attached to my girl or boy. I possess. Is attachment love? Our whole life is based on attachment, attachment to property, attachment to a person, attachment to a belief, to a dogma, to Christ, to Buddha. Is that love? In attachment there is pain, there is fear, there is jealousy, anxiety. Where there is attachment, is there love? When you observe it and you are concerned deeply, most profoundly to find out what love is, then attachment becomes unimportant, it has no value, because that is not love.

It is not desire. It is not remembrance. It is not attachment. It is not that I am telling you and you accept it. It is so. Is love pleasure? It doesn't mean you can't hold the hand of another. You see, desire is the outcome of sensation. Sensation is attached to thought, thought is attached to sensation, and from that sensation there is desire, and that desire wants to fulfil, and we call that love. Is that love? Is attachment love? In attachment there is conflict, there is uncertainty, and the more uncertainty there is, the more there is the fear of loneliness, the more you become attached, possessive, dominating, asserting, demanding, and hence conflict in relationship. And this conflict you think is part of love. We are asking: Is that love?

Is pleasure love? Pleasure is the movement of a remembrance. Don't memorize the phrase, just listen to it. I remember how nice you were and how pleasant, how tender, how comforting, how sexual, and I say, 'Darling, I love you'. Is that love? But is pleasure to be denied? You must ask all these questions. You must ask, find out. Doesn't it give you pleasure to look at the waters of a stream? What is wrong with that pleasure? Doesn't it give you pleasure to look at a solitary tree in a field? Doesn't it give you pleasure to see the moon over the mountains as you perhaps saw it last night? A great delight, wasn't it? What is wrong with it? But the trouble begins when thought says, 'How beautiful this is, I must keep it, I must remember it, I must worship it, I hope to have more of it'. Then the whole movement of pleasure comes into operation. And that pleasure we call love.

The mother with her baby is full of that tender affection, the feeling of holding. Is that love? Or is that love part of your heredity? Have you seen the monkeys holding their babies, the elephant caring for the little one infinitely? It may be that we have inherited this instinctual response to a baby—and then, 'It is *my* baby. It has got my blood, my bones, my flesh, I love it'. And if you do love your baby so greatly, you will see he is properly educated, you will see that he is never violent, he is never killed or kills another. You don't just care for that little baby until it is five or six, and then throw it to the wolves.

So is all this love? Now, the positive action is to say, 'No. I will no longer have sex', 'I will be free of attachment', 'I will work on attachment all the time'. Whereas the negative action is to see it in its entirety and therefore have an insight into it. Then you will see that love is not any of these things, but because there is love, from that love all relationship changes. You know the ascetics, the *sannyasis* in India, the monks in Europe and all over the world have said, 'No desire, no sex, don't look at a beautiful woman. If you do, think of her as your sister or your mother. Or, if you do look, concentrate on the divine'. And they are burning inside! They deny outwardly, but are inwardly burning. And that is what they call a religious life; which means they have no love. They have an idea of what love is. The idea is not love. The idea, the word is not love. But only when you have seen the whole movement of desire, attachment, pleasure, then out of that depth of perception comes this strange flower with its extraordinary perfume. That is love.

Bombay, 31 January 1982

WHAT ARE WE? Apart from a name, a form, perhaps if you are lucky a bank account, perhaps a skill, apart from all that, what are we? Are we not suffering? Or does suffering not exist in your life? Is there fear? Is there anxiety, greed, envy? Do we worship some image which thought has created? Frightened of death, are we clinging to some concept? Aren't we in contradiction, saying one thing and doing another? We are all that. Our habits, our inanities, the endless chatter that goes on in the mind, all that is what we are.

The content of consciousness makes consciousness, and that consciousness has been evolving through time, through tremendous experiences, pains, sorrow. Can one be free of all that, free from all sense of fear? Because where there is fear, there is no love. Sensitiveness cannot exist if there is self-centred activity all the time, and without that sensitivity, there is no love. And there is no love when there is no beauty. Beauty exists only in the flowering of goodness.

Let us look at what beauty is—not the beauty of form, which is also nice, the beauty of a lovely tree, the beauty of a green field, the beauty of a mountain, the majesty of it against the blue sky, the beauty of a sunset, the beauty of a solitary flower growing through the pavement. We are not being romantic, or emotional. We are inquiring together into what beauty is. Do you have that sense of beauty in your life, or is it mediocre, meaningless, an everlasting struggle from morning until night? What is beauty? It isn't a sensual question, nor a sexual question. It is a very serious question because without beauty in your heart, you cannot flower in goodness. Have you ever looked at a mountain or the blue sea without chattering, without making noise, really paid attention to the blue sea, the beauty of water, the beauty of light on a sheet of water. When you see such extraordinary beauty of the earth, with its rivers, lakes, mountains, what actually takes place? What takes place when you look at something which you have seen which is actually marvellously beautiful: a statue, a poem, a lily in the pond, or a well-kept lawn? At that moment, the very majesty of a mountain makes you forget yourself. Have you ever been in that position? If you have, you have seen that then you don't exist, only that grandeur exists. But a few seconds later or a minute later, the whole cycle begins, the confusion, the chatter. So beauty *is*, where you are not. It is a tragedy if you don't see this. Truth *is*, where you are not. Beauty is, love is, where you are not. We are not capable of looking at this extraordinary thing called truth.

Can mankind ever end suffering, not just personal suffering, but the suffering of humanity? Think of all the men and women maimed, hurt in a thousand wars. There is sorrow in the world, a global sorrow, and there is also sorrow of your own; they are not two separate sorrows. Please see this. I may suffer because my son is dead. I am also aware that my neighbour's wife is dead. It is the same throughout the world. It has been like this for millennia, for thousands upon thousands of years, and we have never been able to resolve it. We may escape from it, we may do rituals, ceremonials, we may invent all kinds of theories, say that it is our karma, it is from our past, but suffering is there, not only yours, but that of the whole of humanity. Can that suffering ever end, or is it the condition of humanity that suffering must continue from time immemorial to the ending of time? If you accept that that is the condition—which I hope you don't—then you will continue to suffer endlessly. You get used to it, as most of us do. But if you don't accept that, what is your position? Will you take time to end that suffering? You are the past, the present, and the future. You are that. You are the master of time, and you can shorten the time or lengthen the time. If you are violent and you say, 'I will become non-violent', that is extending time. During that interval of time, you are being violent, and there is no end to that kind of activity. If you realize that you are the master of time, that time is in your hands, which is an extraordinarily important thing to find out, that means you face the fact of violence. You don't pursue non-violence, but face the fact of violence, and in that observation there is no time at all, because in that observation there is neither the observer nor all the past accumulation, there is only pure observation. In that there is no time.

Are you doing this? When the speaker is talking about it, are you actually seeing the truth of it and therefore doing it? Suppose I have a particular habit, physical or psychological; can the habit end immediately? Or will I take time to end a habit? Suppose you smoke; can you end that habit immediately? The craving of the body for nicotine is different from the perception that you are the master of time. You can shorten the time, therefore that perception is not a decision not to smoke.

You see, only when one ends sorrow is there passion. Passion is not lust. Lust is sensual, sexual, it is full of desire, pictures, pursuits of pleasure, and so on. Passion is not. You must have passion to create—not babies—to bring about a different world, different human beings in the world, to change the society in which you live. Without that tremendous passion, one becomes mediocre, soft, unclear, lacking integrity.

My son is dead and I suffer. I shed tears. I go to all the temples in the world. I have put all my hope in that son and he is gone. And I have a craving that he will live somewhere else and I hope I will meet him somewhere in the next life, or somewhere or other. We are always playing with that. Suffering is very painful. Tears, other people's comfort, and my own search for comfort away from that pain, do not resolve the pain, the tremendous sense of loneliness. So can I look at it, be with it, without any kind of escape, without any kind of rational explanation for the death of my son? Without seeking reincarnation or something else, can I remain completely, wholly, with that feeling of great pain? Then what takes place?

I hope you are doing this with the speaker. Don't just listen to it. You are not being told what to do. This is not an intellectual play; this is our life, our daily existence. The person you love may go away, and there is jealousy, anxiety, hatred. This is our life and we suffer.

If my son has died, I can't tolerate the idea that he has gone. Without any sentiment, without any emotion, can I remain with that pain, the pain of loneliness? Most of us know loneliness. That loneliness is when you are totally isolated from all relationship. You suddenly find yourself in a crowd but you are utterly lonely, alone. It is part of sorrow to find such a state. When my son dies, I am lonely. Can I look at loneliness, observe that loneliness without any past memories, and observe without the observer? We will talk about it.

When one is angry, at that moment of anger, which is a reaction, there is neither the observer nor the observed. Have you noticed? There is only that reaction which is called *anger*. A few minutes or a few seconds later, the observer says, 'I have been angry'. So the observer separates himself from anger and then says, 'I have been angry'. But the observer is the observed. Anger is not different from me; I am anger. I am greed. I am frightened. I am all that. But thought says, 'I must control, I must escape from fear', so thought then creates the observer as different from the observed, and in that state there is conflict. Whereas the fact is that the observer is the observed. Anger is you, anger is not different from you. Similarly, when I have lost my son, I am in that state, observing without any movement of thought, which is to give total attention to that thing called *pain*, to that thing called *loneliness* which brings about such despair, such neurotic activity. Can I remain with that sense of intense sorrow, pain, shock, without any single movement or shadow of thought? That is to give complete attention to it. You cannot give complete attention if you are trying to escape from it; that is a waste of energy, whereas if you give your total attention then all the energy is focused on a point which you call suffering. When you do that, you understand the whole significance and the depth and the beauty of such an extraordinary fact. And then suffering ends. When there is the ending of suffering there is passion. And with the ending of suffering there is love.

What is love? Have you ever asked? Have you ever asked your husband or your wife what love is? You daren't! Do I love anybody? Do you know what that means? Is love desire? Is love pleasure? Is love attachment? Please consider all this. Is love jealousy? Or has love now become a sexual act? We are going together to see the quality of a mind or a brain that loves. Do you love your children, or feel responsible for them as your duty? Have you ever considered whether you love your children? You will say, 'Of course', but we are asking this seriously. If you loved your children, would you want them to be what you are? Or would you want them to be totally different from you? Do you want them to follow your trade, your business? Because you are an industrialist, do you want your son to be an industrialist? Or are you concerned that he should grow in goodness, flower in beauty? Or are you preparing him for war, to kill and be killed? Is all that love? I know you will say, 'We can't help what we are. We can't help our children. We send them off to school and that is the end of it'. You only want them to get married, settle down—as you have settled down—in mediocrity, with lack of integrity, saying one thing and doing another, going to the temple and being an excellent lawyer. That is a contradiction. Do you want your children to be like that? If you loved them, would you do this?

Does love exist anywhere in the world? Is love jealousy? Is love attachment? If I am attached to my wife, what a tragedy it all is, isn't it? What are the implications of that attachment? Is that love? If I am attached to her, I depend on her, both physically and psychologically; she helps me, I help her. I am frightened that she may leave me. I am anxious that she shouldn't leave me. She mustn't look at another man, she must remain faithful to me. I must possess her, dominate her. And she wants to be possessed and to be dominated. Is that love in which there is fear, jealousy, hatred, antagonism? Is all that love?

To deny, to negate everything that is not love, is love. So we completely negate jealousy, totally negate attachment, negate every form of possessiveness. Out of that total negation comes love. Through negation you come to the positive. And the most positive thing is love. One of the odd things about love is that whatever you do will be correct if you love. When there is love, action is always right, in all circumstances. And when there is that quality of love, there is compassion. Compassion means passion for all. Compassion cannot exist, nor love, if you belong to any sect, any group, or to any organized religion. Compassion comes only when there is freedom from all that. And that compassion has its own extraordinary, limitless intelligence. When there is love, there is beauty. Love and compassion with their intelligence is the endless truth. To that truth there is no path—not Karma Yoga, Bhakti Yoga, and so on—there is no path to truth. Only when there is that immense sense of compassion that comes when there is the ending of sorrow, then that which is, is truth.

With Young People in India:
From Life Ahead

LET US TALK for a while about love; let us find out whether behind this word and this feeling—which has so much significance for all of us—there is also that peculiar element of apprehension, of anxiety, the thing which grownup people know as loneliness.

Do you know what love is? Do you love your father, your mother, your brother, your teacher, your friend? Do you know what it means to love? When you say that you love your parents, what does it mean? You feel safe with them, you feel at home with them. Your parents are protecting you, they are giving you money, shelter, food and clothing, and you feel with them a sense of close relationship, don't you? You also feel that you can trust them—or you may not. Probably you do not talk to them as easily and happily as you do to your own friends. But you respect them, you are guided by them, you obey them, you have a certain sense of responsibility towards them, feeling that you must support them when they are old. They in turn love you, they want to protect you, to guide you, to help you—at least they say so. They want to marry you off so that you will lead a so-called moral life and stay out of trouble, so that you will have a husband to look after you, or a wife to cook for you and bear your children. All this is called love, is it not?

We cannot immediately say what love is, because love is not readily explained by words. It does not come to us easily. Yet without love, life is very barren; without love, the trees, the birds, the smile of men and women, the bridge across the river, the boatmen and the animals, have no meaning. Without love, life is like a shallow pool. In a deep river, there is richness and many fish can live; but the shallow pool is soon dried up by the strong sun, and nothing remains except mud and dirt.

For most of us, love is an extraordinarily difficult thing to understand because our lives are very shallow. We want to be loved, and also we want to love, and behind that word there is a lurking fear. So is it not very important for each one of us to find out what this extraordinary thing really is? And we can find out only if we are aware of how we regard other human beings, how we look at the trees, at the animals, at a stranger, at the man who is hungry. We must be aware of how we regard our friends, of how we regard our guru, if we have one, of how we regard our parents.

When you say, 'I love my father and my mother, I love my guardian, my teacher', what does it mean? When you respect somebody tremendously and look up to them, when you feel it is your duty to obey them and they in turn expect your obedience, is that love? Is love apprehensive? Surely, when you look up to somebody, you also look down upon somebody else. And is that love? In love is there any sense of looking up or looking down, any compulsion to obey another?

When you say you love somebody, don't you inwardly depend on that person? While you are a child, you naturally depend on your father, on your mother, on your teacher, on your guardian. You need to be cared for, to be provided with food, clothing, and shelter. You need a sense of security, the feeling that someone is looking after you. But what generally happens? As we grow older, this feeling of dependence continues. Haven't you noticed it in older people, in your parents and teachers? Haven't you observed how they depend emotionally on their wives or husbands, on their children, or on their own parents? When they grow up, most people still cling to somebody; they continue to be dependent. Without someone to lean on, to give them a sense of comfort and security, they feel lonely. They feel lost. This dependency on another is called love; but if you observe it very closely, you will see that dependency is fear, it is not love.

Most people are afraid to stand alone; they are afraid to think things out for themselves, afraid to feel deeply, to explore and discover the whole meaning of life. Therefore they say they love God, and they depend on what they call God; but it is not God, the unknown, it is a thing created by the mind.

We do the same with an ideal or a belief. I believe in something, or I hold on to an ideal, and that gives me great comfort; but remove the ideal, remove the belief, and I am lost. It is the same thing with a guru. I depend because I want to receive, so there is the ache of fear. Again, it is the same when you depend on your parents or teachers. It is natural and right that you should do so when you are young; but if you keep on depending when you have grown to maturity, that will make you incapable of thinking, of being free. Where there is dependence, there is fear, and where there is fear, there is authority, there is no love. When your parents say that you must obey, that you must follow certain traditions, that you must take only a certain job or do only a particular kind of work—in all that there is no love. And there is no love in your heart when you depend on society, in the sense that you accept the structure of society as it is, without question.

Ambitious men and women do not know what love is, and we are dominated by ambitious people. That is why there is no happiness in the world, and why it is very important that you, as you grow up, should see and understand all this, and find out for yourself if it is possible to discover what love is. You may have a good position, a very fine house, a marvellous garden, clothes; you may become the prime minister; but without love, none of these things has any meaning.

So you have to begin to find out now—not wait until you are old, for you will never find out then—what it is you actually feel in your relationship with your parents, with your teachers, with the guru. You cannot merely accept the word *love* or any other word, but must go behind the meaning of words to see what the reality is—

the reality being that which you actually feel, not what you are supposed to feel. If you actually feel jealous or angry, to say, 'I must not be jealous, I must not be angry', is merely a wish, it has no reality. What matters is to see very honestly and very clearly exactly what it is you are feeling at the moment, without bringing in the ideal of how you should feel or will feel at some future date, for then you can do something about it. But to say, 'I must love my parents, I must love my teachers', has no meaning. Because your real feelings are quite different, and those words become a screen behind which you hide.

So is it not the way of intelligence to look beyond the accepted meanings of words? Words like *duty, responsibility, God, love,* have acquired a traditional meaning; but an intelligent person, a truly educated person, looks beyond the traditional meaning of such words. For instance, if someone told you that he did not believe in God, you would be shocked, would you not? You would say, 'Goodness, how awful', because you believe in God—at least you think you do. But belief and non-belief have very little meaning. What is important is for you to go behind the word *love* to see whether you actually do love your parents, and whether your parents actually do love you. Surely, if you and your parents really loved one another, the world would be entirely different. There would be no wars, no starvation, no class differences. There would be no rich and no poor. You see, without love we try to reform society economically, we try to put things right; but as long as we have no love in our hearts, we cannot bring about a social structure free of conflict and misery. That is why we have to go into these things very carefully; and perhaps then we shall find out what love is.

Questioner: Why is there sorrow and misery in the world?

Krishnamurti: I wonder if that boy knows what those words mean. He has probably seen an over-loaded donkey with his legs almost breaking, or another boy crying, or a mother beating her child. Perhaps he has seen older people quarrelling with each other. And there is death, the body being carried away to be burned; there is the beggar; there is poverty, disease, old age; there is sorrow, not only outside, but also inside us. So he asks, 'Why is there sorrow?' Don't you want to know too? Have you never wondered about the cause of your own sorrow? What is sorrow, and why does it exist? If I want something and cannot get it, I feel miserable; if I want more saris, more money, or if I want to be more beautiful, and cannot have what I want, I am unhappy. If I want to love a certain person and that person does not love me, again I am miserable. My father dies, and I am in sorrow. Why?

Why do we feel unhappy when we cannot have what we want? Why should we necessarily have what we want? We think it is our right, do we not? But do we ever ask ourselves why we should have what we want when millions have not got even what they need? And besides, why do we want it? There is our need of food, clothing, and shelter; but we are not satisfied with that. We want much more. We want success, we want to be respected, loved, looked up to, we want to be powerful, we want to be famous poets, saints, orators, we want to be prime ministers, presidents. Why? Have you ever looked into it? Why do we want all this? Not that we must be satisfied with what we are. I do not mean that. That would be ugly, silly. But why this constant craving for more and more and more? This craving indicates that we are dissatisfied, discontented; but with what? With what we are? I am this, I do not like it, and I want to be that. I think I shall look much more beautiful in a new coat or a new sari, so I want it. This means I am dissatisfied with what I am, and I think I can escape from my discontent by acquiring more clothes, more power, and so on. But the dissatisfaction is still there, is it not? I have only covered it up with clothes, with power, with cars.

So we have to find out how to understand what we are. Merely to cover ourselves with possessions, with power and position, has no meaning, because we will still be unhappy. Seeing this, the unhappy person, the person who is in sorrow, does not run away to gurus, he does not hide in possessions, in power; on the contrary, he wants to know what lies behind his sorrow. If you go behind your own sorrow, you will find that you are very small, empty, limited, and that you are struggling to achieve, to become. This very struggle to achieve, to become something, is the cause of sorrow. But if you begin to understand what you actually are, go deeper and deeper into it, then you will find that something quite different takes place.

Q: If a man is starving and I feel that I can be helpful to him, is this ambition or love?

K: It all depends on the motive with which you help him. By saying he is for helping the poor man, the politician gets to New Delhi, lives in a big house, and shows himself off. Is that love? Do you understand? Is that love?

Q: If I relieve his starvation by my helpfulness, isn't that love?

K: He is starving and you help him with food. Is that love? Why do you want to help him? Have you no motive, no incentive other than the desire to help him? Do you not get any benefit out of it? Think this out, do not say yes or no. If you are looking for some benefit out of it, politically or otherwise, some inward or outward benefit, then you do not love him. If you feed him in order to become more popular, or in the hope that your friends will help you to go to New Delhi, then that is not love, is it? But if you love him, you will feed him without any ulterior motive, without wanting anything in return. If you feed him and he is ungrateful, do you feel hurt? If so, you do not love him. If he tells you and the villagers that you are a wonderful man, and you feel very flattered, it means you are thinking about yourself; and surely that is not love. So one has to be very alert to find out if one is deriving any kind of benefit from one's helpfulness, and what the motive is that leads one to feed the hungry.

Saanen, 18 July 1968:
From Talks and Dialogues in Saanen 1968

To explore pleasure, that very important factor in life, we have also to understand what love is, and in understanding that we have also to find out what beauty is. So there are three things involved: there is pleasure; there is beauty, about which we talk and feel a great deal; and there is love—that word which is so spoiled. We will go into it step by step, rather diligently yet hesitantly, because such a vast field of human existence is covered by these three things. And to come to any conclusion, to say 'This is pleasure', or 'One must not have pleasure', or 'This is love', 'This is beauty', seems to me to demand the very clearest comprehension and feeling of beauty, of love, and of pleasure. So we must, if we are somewhat wise, avoid any formula, any conclusion, any definite apprehension about this deep subject. To come into contact with the deep truth of these three things is not a matter of intellection nor of the definition of words, nor of any vague, mystical, or parapsychological feeling.

For most of us, pleasure and its expression are very important. Most of our moral values are based on it, on the ultimate or immediate pleasure; our hereditary and psychological trends and our physical and neurological reactions are based on pleasure. If you examine not only the outward values and judgments of society, but also look within yourself, you will see that pleasure and its evaluation is the main pursuit of our lives. We may resist, we may sacrifice, we may achieve or deny, but at the end of it there is always this sense of gaining pleasure, satisfaction, contentment, of being pleased or gratified. Self-expression and self-fulfilment is a form of pleasure; and when that pleasure is thwarted, blocked, there is fear, and out of that fear there is aggression.

Please, watch this in yourself. You are not just listening to a lot of words or ideas; they have no meaning. You can read in a book a psychological explanation that will have no value. But if we investigate together, step by step, then you will see for yourself what an extraordinary thing comes out of it.

Bear in mind that we are not saying we must not have pleasure, that pleasure is wrong, as the various religious groups throughout the world maintain. We are not saying you must suppress, deny, control, translate to a higher level, and all that kind of thing. We are just examining. And if we can examine quite objectively, deeply, then out of that comes a different state of mind which has a bliss, but not pleasure; bliss is something entirely different.

We know what pleasure is: looking at a beautiful mountain, at a lovely tree, at the light in a cloud that is chased by the wind across the sky, at the beauty of the river with its clear running water. There is a great deal of pleasure in watching all of this or in seeing the beautiful face of a woman, a man, or a child. We all know the pleasure that comes through touch, taste, seeing, listening. And when that intense pleasure is sustained by thought, then there is the counteraction which is aggression, reprisal, anger, hate, born out of the feeling of not getting that pleasure which you are after, and therefore fear, which is again fairly obvious if you observe it. Any kind of experience is sustained by thought, the pleasure of an experience of yesterday, whatever it was, sensual, sexual, visual. Thought thinks over, thought chews over the pleasure, goes over it, creating an image or picture which sustains it, gives it nourishment. Thought gives sustenance to that pleasure of yesterday, gives it a continuity today and tomorrow. Do notice it. And when the pleasure sustained by that thought is inhibited, because it is bound round by circumstance, by various forms of hindrances, then thought is in revolt, it turns its energy into aggression, into hate, into violence, which again is another form of pleasure.

Most of us seek pleasure through self-expression. We want to express ourselves, whether in little or in great things. The artist wants to express himself on the canvas, the author in books, the musician using an instrument, and so on. Is this self-expression—from which one derives an enormous amount of pleasure—beauty? When an artist expresses himself, he derives pleasure and intense satisfaction. Is that beauty? Or, because he can't completely convey on canvas or in words what he feels, is there discontent, which is another form of pleasure?

So is beauty pleasure? When there is self-expression in any form, does it convey beauty? Is love pleasure? Love has now almost become synonymous with sex and its expression and all that is involved in it—self-forgetfulness and so on. When thought derives intense pleasure from something, is that love? When it is thwarted it becomes jealousy, anger, hatred. Pleasure entails domination, possession, dependence, and therefore fear. So one asks oneself, is love pleasure? Is love desire in all its subtle forms—for sex, for companionship, for tenderness, for self-forgetfulness? Is all that love, and if it is not, then what is love?

If you have observed your own mind operating, being aware of the very activity of the brain, you will see that from ancient times, from the very beginning, man has pursued pleasure. If you have watched the animal, you see how pleasure is an extraordinarily important thing, and the pursuit of pleasure and the aggression when that pleasure is thwarted.

We are built on that; our judgments, our values, our social demands, our relationships, and so on, are based on this essential principle of pleasure and its self-expression. And when that is thwarted, when that is controlled, twisted, prevented, then there is anger, then there is aggression, which becomes another form of pleasure.

What relationship has pleasure to love? Or has pleasure relationship to love at all? Is love something entirely different? Is love something which is not fragmented by society, by religion—as profane and divine? How are you going to find out? How are you going to find out for yourself, not be told by another? If somebody tells you what it is and you say, 'Yes, that's right', it is not yours, it is not something you have discovered and felt profoundly for yourself.

What relationship has the pleasure of self-expression to beauty and to love? A scientist, a philosopher, a technologist must know the truth of things. For a human being concerned with daily life, with the earning of a livelihood, with the family, and so on, is truth something static? Or is it something that is never stationary, never permanent, but always moving that you discover as you go along? Truth is not an intellectual phenomenon, it is not an emotional or sentimental affair. And we have to find the truth of pleasure, the truth of beauty, and the reality of what love is.

One has seen the torture of love, the dependence on it, the fear of it, the loneliness of not being loved, and the everlasting seeking of it in all kinds of relationships, never finding it to one's complete satisfaction. So one asks, is love satisfaction and, at the same time, a torture hedged about by jealousy, envy, hatred, anger, dependence?

When there is not beauty in the heart, we go to museums and concerts. We marvel at the beauty of an ancient Greek temple with its lovely columns, its proportions against the blue sky. We talk endlessly about beauty; we lose touch with nature altogether as modern man, living more and more in towns. There are societies formed to go into the country to look at the birds, trees, and rivers, as though by forming societies to look at trees you are going to touch nature and come into extraordinary contact with that immense beauty! It is because we have lost touch with nature that paintings, museums, and concerts assume such importance.

There is an emptiness, a sense of inward void that is always seeking self-expression and pleasure, and hence breeding the fear of not having it completely, and so there is resistance, aggression. We proceed to fill that inward void, that emptiness and sense of utter isolation and loneliness—which I am sure you have felt—with books, with knowledge, with relationships, with every form of trickery; but at the end of it, there is still this unfillable emptiness. Then we turn to God, the ultimate resort. When there is this emptiness and this sense of deep, unfathomable void, is love, is beauty, possible? If one is aware of this emptiness and does not escape from it, then what is one to do? We have tried to fill it with gods, with knowledge, with experience, with music, with pictures, with extraordinary technological information; that is what we are occupied with morning until night. When one realizes that this emptiness cannot be filled by any person, one sees the importance of this. If you fill it with what is called *relationship* with another person, or with an image, then out of that comes dependence and the fear of loss, then aggressive possession, jealousy, and all that follows. So one asks oneself: Can that emptiness ever be filled by anything, by social activity, good works, going to a monastery and meditating, training oneself to be aware?—which is such an absurdity. If one cannot fill it, then what is one to do? You understand the importance of this question? One has tried to fill it with what one calls pleasure, through self-expression, searching for truth, God; one realizes that nothing can ever fill it, neither the image one has created about oneself nor the image or ideology one has created about the world, nothing. And so one has used beauty, love, and pleasure to cover this emptiness, and if one no longer escapes but remains with it, then what is one to do?

What is this loneliness, this sense of deep inward void? What is it and how does it come into being? Does it exist because we are trying to fill it, or are trying to escape from it? Does it exist because we are afraid of it? Is it just an idea of emptiness, and therefore the mind is never in contact with what actually is, is never directly in relationship with it?

I discover this emptiness in myself and I cease to escape, for that is obviously an immature activity. I am aware of it, there it is and nothing can fill it. Now, I ask myself: How has this come into being? Has all my living, all my daily activities and assumptions, and so on, produced it? Is it that the *self*, the *me*, the *ego*, or whatever word you may use, is isolating itself in all its activity? The very nature of the 'me', the 'self', the 'ego', is isolation; it is separative. All these activities have produced this isolated state, this state of deep emptiness in myself; so it is a result, a consequence, not something inherent. I see that as long as my activity is self-centred and self-expressive, there must be this void, and I see that, to fill this void, I make every kind of effort; which again is self-centred, and the emptiness becomes wider and deeper.

Is it possible to go beyond this state? Not by escaping from it, not by saying, 'I will not be self-centred'. When one says 'I will not be self-centred', one is already self-centred. When one exercises will to deny the activity of the self, that very will is the factor of isolation.

The mind has been conditioned through centuries upon centuries in its demand for security and safety; it has built both physiologically and psychologically this self-centred activity; and this activity pervades daily life—*my* family, *my* job, *my* possessions—and that produces this emptiness, this isolation. How is that activity to end? Can it ever end, or must one entirely ignore that activity and bring another quality to it altogether?

So I see this emptiness, I see how it has come into being, I am aware that will or any other activity exerted to dispel the creator of this emptiness is only another form of self-centred activity. I see all that very clearly, objectively, and I realize suddenly that I cannot do anything about it. Before, I did something about it: I escaped, or I tried to fill it, I tried to understand it, to go into it, but they are all other forms of isolation. So I suddenly realize that I cannot do anything, that the more I try to do something about it, the more I am creating and building walls of isolation. The mind itself realizes that it cannot do anything about it, that thought cannot touch it, because the moment thought touches it, it breeds emptiness again. So by carefully observing, objectively, I see this whole process, and the very seeing of it is enough. See what has happened. Before, I used energy to fill this emptiness, wandered all over the place, and now I see the absurdity of it—the mind sees very clearly how absurd it is. So now I am not dissipating energy. Thought becomes quiet; the mind becomes completely still; it has seen the whole map of this and so there is silence. In that silence there is no loneliness. When there is that silence, that complete silence of the mind, there is beauty and love, which may or may not express itself.

Have we taken the journey together? What we are talking about is one of the most difficult things and one of the most dangerous, because if you are at all neurotic, as most of us are, then it becomes complicated and ugly. It is a tremendously complex problem; but when you look at it, it becomes very, very simple, and the very simplicity of it leads you to think you have got it.

So there is bliss only, which is beyond pleasure; there is beauty, which is not the expression of a cunning mind, but the beauty that is known when the mind is completely silent. It is raining and you can hear the patter of the drops. You can hear it with your ears, or you can hear it out of that deep silence. If you hear it with complete silence of the mind, then the beauty of it is such that cannot be put into words or onto canvas, because that beauty is something beyond self-expression. Love, obviously, is bliss, which is not pleasure.

Saanen, 5 August 1962

I WOULD LIKE, IF I may, to talk about the ending of sorrow, because fear, sorrow, and what we call love, always go together. Unless we understand fear, we shall not be able to understand sorrow, nor can we know that state of love in which there is no contradiction, no friction.

To end sorrow completely is a most difficult thing to do, for sorrow is always with us in one form or another. So I would like to go into this problem rather deeply; but my words will have very little meaning unless each one of us examines the problem within himself, neither agreeing nor disagreeing, but simply observing the fact. If we can do this, actually and not just theoretically, then perhaps we shall be able to understand the enormous significance of sorrow and thereby put an end to sorrow.

Throughout the centuries love and sorrow have always gone hand in hand, sometimes one predominating, and sometimes the other. That state which we call love soon passes away, and again we are caught up in our jealousies, our vanities, our fears, our miseries. There has always been this battle between love and sorrow; and before we can go into the question of ending sorrow, I think we must understand what passion is.

❖

PASSION IS SOMETHING WHICH very few of us have really felt. What we may have felt is enthusiasm, which is being caught up in an emotional state over something. Our passion is *for* something: for music, for painting, for literature, for a country, for a woman or a man; it is always the effect of a cause. When you fall in love with someone, you are in a great state of emotion, which is the effect of that particular cause; and what I am talking about is passion without a cause. It is to be passionate about everything, not just about something, whereas most of us are passionate about a particular person or thing. I think one must see this distinction very clearly.

In the state of passion without a cause, there is intensity free of all attachment; but when passion has a cause, there is attachment, and attachment is the beginning of sorrow. Most of us are attached; we cling to a person, to a country, to a belief, to an idea, and when the object of our attachment is taken away or otherwise loses its significance, we find ourselves empty, insufficient. This emptiness we try to fill by clinging to something else, which again becomes the object of our passion.

Please examine your own heart and mind. I am merely a mirror in which you are looking at yourself. If you don't want to look, that is quite all right, but if you do want to look, then look at yourself clearly, ruthlessly, with intensity—not in the hope of dissolving your miseries, your anxieties, your sense of guilt, but in order to understand this extraordinary passion which always leads to sorrow.

When passion has a cause, it becomes lust. When there is a passion for something—for a person, for an idea, for some kind of fulfilment—then out of that passion there comes contradiction, conflict, effort. You strive to achieve or maintain a particular state, or to recapture one that has been and is gone. But the passion of which I am speaking does not give rise to contradiction, conflict. It is totally unrelated to a cause, and therefore it is not an effect.

Just listen; don't try to achieve this state of intensity, this passion without a cause. If we can listen attentively, with that sense of ease which comes when attention is not forced through discipline but is born of the simple urge to understand, then I think we shall find out for ourselves what this passion is.

In most of us there is very little passion. We may be lustful, we may be longing for something, we may be wanting to escape from something, and all this does give one a certain intensity. But unless we awaken and feel our way into this flame of passion without a cause, we shall not be able to understand that which we call sorrow. To understand something, you must have passion, the intensity of complete attention. Where there is the passion for something—which produces contradiction, conflict—this pure flame of passion cannot be; and this pure flame of passion must exist in order to end sorrow, dissipate it completely.

We know that sorrow is a result; it is the effect of a cause. I love somebody and that person doesn't love me—that is one kind of sorrow. I want to fulfil myself in a certain direction, but I haven't got the capacity; or if I have the capacity, ill health or some other factor blocks my fulfilment—that is another form of sorrow. There is the sorrow of a petty mind, of a mind that is always in conflict with itself, incessantly struggling, adjusting, groping, conforming. There is the sorrow of conflict in relationship, and the sorrow of losing someone by death. You all know these various forms of sorrow, and they are all the result of a cause.

Now, we never face the fact of sorrow; we are always trying to rationalize it, explain it away; or we cling to a dogma, a pattern of belief which satisfies us, gives us momentary comfort. Some take a drug, others turn to drink, or to prayer—anything to lessen the intensity, the agony of sorrow. Sorrow, and the everlasting attempt to escape from sorrow, is the lot of each one of us. We have never thought of ending sorrow completely, so that the mind is not at any time caught in self-pity, in the shadow of despair. Not being able to end sorrow, if we are Christians, we worship it in our churches as the agony of Christ. And whether we go to church and worship the symbol of sorrow, or try to rationalize sorrow away, or forget our sorrow by taking a drink, it is all the same: We are escaping from the fact that we suffer. I am not talking about physical pain, which can be dealt with fairly easily by modern medicine. I am talking about sorrow, the psychological pain that prevents clarity, beauty, that destroys love and compassion. Is it possible to bring all sorrow to an end? I think the ending of sorrow is related to the intensity of passion. There can be passion only when there is total self-abandonment. One is never passionate unless there is a complete absence of what we call thought. What we call thought is the response of the various patterns and experiences of memory, and where this conditioned response exists, there is no passion, there is no intensity. There can be intensity only when there is a complete absence of the 'me'.

You know, there is a sense of beauty which is not concerned with what is beautiful and what is ugly. Not that the mountain is not beautiful, or that there is not an ugly building, but there is beauty which is not the opposite of ugliness, there is love which is not the opposite of hate. And the self-abandonment of which I am speaking is that state of beauty without cause, and therefore it is a state of passion. Is it possible to go beyond that which is the result of a cause?

Please do give complete attention, to gather the meaning rather than stay with the words.

You see, most of us are always reacting; reaction is the whole pattern of our life. Our response to sorrow is a reaction. We respond by trying to explain the cause of sorrow, or by escaping from sorrow, but our sorrow doesn't end. Sorrow ends only when we face the fact of sorrow, when we understand and go beyond both the cause and the effect. To try to be free of sorrow through a particular practice, or by deliberate thought, or by indulging in any of the various ways of escaping from sorrow, doesn't awaken in the mind the extraordinary beauty, the vitality, the intensity of that passion which includes and transcends sorrow.

What is sorrow? When you hear this question, how do you respond? Your mind immediately tries to explain the cause of sorrow, and this seeking of an explanation awakens the memory of the sorrows you have had. So you are always verbally reverting to the past or going forward to the future in an effort to explain the cause of the effect which we call sorrow. But I think one has to go beyond all that.

We know very well what causes sorrow—poverty, ill-health, frustration, the lack of being loved, and so on. And when we have explained the various causes of sorrow, we haven't ended sorrow; we haven't really grasped the extraordinary depth and significance of sorrow any more than we have understood that state which we call love. I think the two are related—sorrow and love—and to understand what love is, one has to feel the immensity of sorrow.

The ancients talked about the ending of sorrow, and they laid down a way of life that is supposed to end sorrow. Many people have practised that way of life. Monks in the East and in the West have tried it, but they have only hardened themselves; their minds and their hearts have become enclosed. They live behind the walls of their own thought, or behind walls of brick and stone, but I really do not believe they have gone beyond and felt the immensity of this thing called sorrow.

To end sorrow is to face the fact of one's loneliness, one's attachment, one's petty little demand for fame, one's hunger to be loved; it is to be free of self-concern and the puerility of self-pity. And when one has gone beyond all that and has perhaps ended one's personal sorrow, there is still the immense collective sorrow, the sorrow of the world. One may end one's own sorrow by facing in oneself the fact and the cause of sorrow—and that must take place for a mind that would be completely free. But when one has finished with all that, there is still the sorrow of extraordinary ignorance that exists in the world—not the lack of information, of book knowledge, but man's ignorance of himself. The lack of understanding of oneself is the essence of ignorance, which brings about this immensity of sorrow that exists throughout the world. And what actually is sorrow?

You see, there are no words to explain sorrow, any more than there are words to explain what love is. Love is not attachment, love is not the opposite of hate, love is not jealousy. And when one has finished with jealousy, with envy, with attachment, with all the conflicts and the agonies one goes through, thinking that one loves—when all that has come to an end, there still remains the question of what is love, and there still remains the question of what is sorrow.

You will find out what love is, and what sorrow is, only when your mind has rejected all explanations and is no longer imagining, no longer seeking the cause, no longer indulging in words or going back in memory to its own pleasures and pains. Your mind must be completely quiet, without a word, without a symbol, without an idea. And then you will discover—or there will come into being—that state in which what we have called love and what we have called sorrow and what we have called death are the same. There is no longer any division between love and sorrow and death; and there being no division, there is beauty. But to comprehend, to be in this state of ecstasy, there must be that passion which comes with the total abandonment of oneself.

Bombay, 21 February 1965

To UNDERSTAND PLEASURE, we must come to it to learn, not to suppress it, not to indulge in it. To learn about it is a discipline, which demands that you neither indulge nor deny. The learning comes when you understand that if there is any form of suppression, denial, control, you cease to learn, there is no learning. Therefore, to understand the whole problem of pleasure, you must come to it with a fresh mind. For us, pleasure is extraordinarily important. We do things out of pleasure. We run away from anything that is painful, and we reduce things to the values, to the criteria of pleasure. So pleasure plays an extraordinarily important part in our life, as an ideal, as a man who gives up this so-called worldly life to find another kind of life—it is still the basis of pleasure. Or when people say, 'I must help the poor', and indulge in social reform, it is still an act of pleasure; they may cover it up by calling it *service, goodness*, and so on, but it is still a movement of the mind that is seeking pleasure or escaping from anything that causes a disturbance which it calls *pain*. If you observe yourself, this is what we are doing in daily life, every moment. You like somebody because he flatters you, and you do not like another because she says something which is true and which you do not like, and you create an antagonism; and therefore you live with a constant battle.

So it is very important to understand this thing called *pleasure*. I mean by *understand*, to learn about it. There is a great deal to learn, because all our sensory reactions, all the values that we have created, all the demands—the so-called self-sacrifice, the denial, the acceptance—are based on this extraordinary thing, a refined or a crude form of pleasure. We commit ourselves to various activities—as Communists, as socialists, or what you will—on this basis because we think that by identifying ourselves with a particular activity, with a particular idea, with a particular pattern of life, we shall have greater pleasure, we shall derive a greater benefit; and that value, that benefit, is based on the identification of ourselves with a particular form of activity as pleasure. Please observe all this.

You are not listening to the words merely, but actually listening to find out the truth or the falseness of what is being said. It is your life; it is your everyday life. Most of us waste this extraordinary thing called *life*. We have lived forty or sixty years, have gone to the office, have engaged ourselves in social activity, escaping in various forms, and at the end of it, we have nothing but an empty, dull, stupid life, a wasted life. And that is why it is very important, if you would begin anew, to understand this issue of pleasure. Because the suppressing or the denying of pleasure does not solve the problem of pleasure. The so-called religious people suppress every form of pleasure, at least they attempt it, and therefore they become dull, starved, human beings. And such a mind is arid, dull, insensitive, and cannot possibly find out what is the real.

So it is very important to understand the activities of pleasure. To look at a beautiful tree is a lovely thing; it is a great delight—what is wrong with that? But to look at a woman or a man with pleasure—you call that immoral, because to you pleasure is always involved in, or related to, that one thing, the woman or the man; or it is the escape from the pains of relationship, and therefore you seek pleasure elsewhere, in an idea, in an escape, in a certain activity.

Now, pleasure has created this pattern of social life. We take pleasure in ambition, in competition, in comparing, in acquiring knowledge or power, or position, prestige, status. And that pursuit of pleasure as ambition, competition, greed, envy, status, domination, power is respectable. It is made respectable by a society which has only one concept: that you shall lead a moral life, which is a respectable life. You can be ambitious, you can be greedy, you can be violent, you can be competitive, you can be a ruthless human being, but society accepts it, because, at the end of your ambition, you are either a so-called successful man with plenty of money, or a failure and therefore a frustrated human being. So social morality is immorality.

Please listen to all this, neither agreeing nor disagreeing; see the fact. And to see the fact—that is, to understand the fact—don't evolve ideas about it, don't have opinions about it. You are learning about it, and to learn you must come with a mind that is inquiring and therefore passionate, eager, and therefore young. Morality, which is custom, which is habit, is considered respectable within the pattern as long as you are conforming to the pattern. There are people who revolt against that pattern—this is happening all the time. Revolt is a reaction to the pattern. This reaction takes many forms—the beatniks, the Beatles, the Teddy Boys, and so on—but they are still within the pattern. To be really moral is quite a different thing. And that is why one has to understand the nature of virtue and the nature of pleasure. Our social custom, habit, tradition, relationship—all this is based on pleasure. I am not using that word *pleasure* in a small sense, in a limited sense; I am using it in its widest sense. Our society is based on pleasure, and all our relationship is based on that. You are my friend as long as I comply with what you like, as long as I help you to get better business, but the moment I criticize you, I am not your friend. It is so obvious and silly.

Without understanding pleasure, you will never be able to understand love. Love is not pleasure. Love is something entirely different. And to understand pleasure you have to learn about it. Now, for most of us, or for every human being, sex is a problem. Why? Listen to this very carefully. Because you are not able to solve it, you run away from it. The *sannyasi* runs away from it by taking a vow of celibacy, by denying. Please see what happens to such a mind. By denying something which is a part of your whole structure—the glands and so on—by suppressing it you have made yourself arid, and there is a constant battle going on within yourself.

As we were saying, we have only two ways of meeting any problem, apparently, either suppressing it or running away from it. Suppressing it is really the same thing as running away from it, and we have a whole network of escapes—very intricate, intellectual, emotional—and ordinary everyday activity. There are various forms of escapes. But we have this problem. The sannyasi escapes from it in one way, but he has not resolved it; he has suppressed it by taking a vow, and the whole problem is boiling in him. He may put on the outward robe of simplicity, but this becomes an extraordinary issue for him too, as it is for the man who lives an ordinary life.

How do you solve that problem? You must solve it. It is an act of pleasure. You must understand it. How do you solve it? If you don't solve it, then you merely become caught in a habit. It means a routine; your mind becomes dull, stupid, heavy; and that is the only thing you have. So you have to solve the problem. First of all, do not condemn it, as you are going to learn about it. Please learn about it. That is why we talk about learning. You are throttled intellectually, emotionally; you have merely a repetitive mind; you copy, you imitate what other people have done; you endlessly quote the Gita, or the Upanishads, or some sacred book, but intellectually you are starved, empty, dull. In your office you are intellectually imitating, copying day after day, doing the same thing in your office, or in your factory, or in your home—the constant repetition. So the intellect, which must be vital, clear, reasonable, healthy, free, has been smothered. There is no outlet there, there is no creative action there. Emotionally, aesthetically, you are starved, because you deny emotion with sensitivity, sensitivity to see beauty, to enjoy the loveliness of an evening, to look at a tree and be intimately in communion with nature. So what have you left? You have only one thing in life that is your own; and it becomes an immense problem.

So a mind that would understand that problem must deal with it immediately, because any problem that goes on day after day dulls the spirit, dulls the mind. Haven't you noticed what happens to a mind that has a problem which it is not capable of resolving? Either it is going to escape into some other problem, or it suppresses it, and therefore it becomes neurotic—so-called sanely neurotic, but it is neurotic. So each problem, whatever it is—emotional, intellectual, physical—must be resolved immediately and not carried over to the next day, because the next day you have other problems to meet.

Therefore you have to learn. But you cannot learn if you have not resolved the problems of today, and you merely carry them over to tomorrow. So each problem, however intricate, however difficult, however demanding, must be resolved on the day, on the instant. Please see the importance of this. A mind that gives root to a problem because it has not been able to tackle it, because it has not the capacity, has not the intensity, has not the drive to learn—such a mind as you see in this world—becomes insensitive, fearful, ugly, concerned with itself, self-centred, brutal.

So this problem of so-called sex must be solved. And to solve it intelligently—not run away from it, or suppress it, or take a vow of some idiocy, or indulge in it—one has to understand this problem of pleasure. And also one has to understand another issue, which is that most human beings are second-hand people. You can quote the Gita backwards, but you are a second-hand human being. You have nothing original. There is nothing in you which is spontaneous, real, either intellectually, or aesthetically, or morally. And there is only one thing left—hunger, appetite as food and sex. There is compulsive eating and compulsive sex. You have observed people eating, gorging themselves—and the same thing, sexually.

So to understand this very complex problem—because in that is involved beauty, affection, love—you have to understand pleasure, and to break through this conditioning of a mind that is repetitive, a mind that merely repeats what others have said for centuries or ten years ago. It is a marvellous escape to quote Marx or Stalin or Lenin, and it is a marvellous escape to quote the Gita as though you have understood any of it at all. You have to live; and to live you cannot have problems.

To understand this problem of sex, you must free the mind, the intellect, so that it can look, understand, and move; and also emotionally, aesthetically, you have to look at the trees, the mountains, and the rivers, the squalor of a filthy street, be aware of your children, how they are brought up, how they are dressed, how you treat them, how you talk to them. You have to see the beauty of a line, of a building, of a mountain, of the curve of a river, to see the beauty of a face. All that is the releasing of that energy—not through suppression, not through identification with some idea, but it is the releasing of energy in all directions—so that your mind is active, aesthetically, intellectually, with reason, with clarity, seeing things as they are. The beauty of a tree, of a bird on the wing, the light on the water, and the many other things in life—when you are not aware of all that, naturally, you have only this problem.

Society says that you must be moral, and that morality is the family. The family becomes deadening when it is confined to the family; that is, the family is the individual, and the individual which is the family is opposed to the many, to the collective, to society; then there begins the whole destructive process. So virtue has nothing whatsoever to do with respectability. Virtue is something like a flower that is flowering; that is not a state that you have achieved. You know goodness; you cannot achieve goodness, you cannot achieve humility. It is only the vain man that struggles to become humble. Either you are, or you are not, good. The 'being' is not the 'becoming'. You cannot become good, you cannot become humble. And so it is with virtue. The moral structure of a society which is based on imitation, fear, ugly personal demands and ambitions, greed, envy, is not virtue—nor is it moral. Virtue is the spontaneous action of love—spontaneous, not a calculated, cultivated thing called *virtue*. It must be spontaneous; otherwise, it is not virtue. How can it be virtue if it is a calculated thing, if it is practised, if it is a mechanical thing?

So you have to understand pleasure and you have also to understand the nature and significance of pleasure and sorrow. And you also have to understand virtue and love.

Now, love is something that cannot be cultivated. You cannot say, 'I will learn, I will practise love'. Most idealists, most people who are escaping from themselves through various forms of intellectual, emotional activities, have no love. They may be marvellous social reformers, excellent politicians—if there is such a thing as an 'excellent politician'—but they have no love at all. Love is something entirely different from pleasure. But you cannot come upon love without understanding it with the depth of passion—not denying it, not running away from it, but understanding it. There is a great delight in the beauty of pleasure.

So love is not to be cultivated. Love cannot be divided into divine and physical; it is only love. And it is not that you love the many or the one; that again is an absurd question to ask—'Do you love all?' You know, a flower that has perfume is not concerned who comes to smell it, or who turns his back upon it. So it is with love. Love is not a memory. Love is not a thing of the mind or the intellect. But it comes into being naturally as compassion, when this whole problem of existence—as fear, greed, envy, despair, hope—has been understood and resolved. An ambitious man cannot love. A man who is attached to his family has no love. Nor has jealousy anything to do with love. When you say, 'I love my wife', you really do not mean it, because the next moment you are jealous of her.

Love implies great freedom, but not to do what you like. Love comes only when the mind is very quiet, disinterested, not self-centred. These are not ideals. If you have no love—do what you will, go after all the gods on earth, do all the social activities, try to reform the poor, enter politics, write books, write poems—you are a dead human being. Without love your problems will increase, multiply endlessly. And with love, do what you will, there is no risk, there is no conflict. Then love is the essence of virtue. A mind that is not in a state of love is not a religious mind at all; and it is only the religious mind that is freed from problems, and that knows the beauty of love and truth.

London, 7 April 1953

Questioner: I feel very lonely, and long for some intimate human relationship. Since I can find no companion, what am I to do?

Krishnamurti: One of our difficulties is, surely, that we want to be happy through something, through a person, through a symbol, through an idea, through virtue, through action, through companionship. We think happiness, or reality, or what you like to call it, can be found through something. Therefore we feel that through action, through companionship, through certain ideas, we will find happiness.

So being lonely, I want to find someone or some idea through which I can be happy. But loneliness always remains; it is ever there, under cover. But as it frightens me, and as I do not know what the inward nature of this loneliness is, therefore I want to find something to which to cling. So I think that through something, through a person, I will be happy. So our mind is always concerned with finding something. Through furniture, through a house, through books, through people, through ideas, through rituals, through symbols, we hope to get something, to find happiness. And so the things, the people, the ideas, become extraordinarily important, because through them we hope we shall find it. So we begin to be dependent on them.

But with it all there is still this thing not understood, not resolved; the anxiety, the fear, is still there. And even when I see that it is still there, then I want to use it, to go through, to find what is beyond. So my mind uses everything as a means to go beyond, and so makes everything trivial. If I use you for my fulfilment for my happiness, you become very unimportant, because it is my happiness I am concerned with. So when the mind is concerned with the idea that it can have happiness through somebody, through a thing or through an idea, do I not make all these means transitory? Because my concern is then something else, to go further, to catch something beyond.

Is it not very important that I should understand this loneliness, this ache, this pain of extraordinary emptiness? Because if I understand that, perhaps I shall not use anything to find happiness, I shall not use God as a means to acquire peace, or a ritual in order to have more sensations, exaltations, inspirations. The thing which is eating my heart out is this sense of fear, my loneliness, my emptiness. Can I understand that? Can I resolve that? Most of us are lonely, are we not? Do what we will, radio, books, politics, religion, none of these can really cover that loneliness. I may be socially active, I may identify myself with certain organized philosophies, but whatever I do it is still there, deep down in my unconscious, or in the deeper depths of my being.

How am I to deal with it? How am I to bring it out and completely resolve it? Again, my whole tendency is to condemn, is it not? The thing which I do not know, I am afraid of, and the fear is the outcome of condemnation. After all, I do not know the quality of loneliness, what it actually is. But my mind has judged it by saying it is fearful. It has opinions about the fact, it has ideas about loneliness. And it is these ideas, opinions, that create the fear and prevent me from really looking at that loneliness.

I hope I am making myself clear? I am lonely; and I am afraid of it. What causes the fear? Isn't it that I do not know the implications involved in loneliness? If I knew the content of loneliness, then I would not be afraid of it. But because I have an idea of what it might be, I run away from it. The very running away creates the fear, not the looking at it. To look at it, to be with it, I cannot condemn. And when I am capable of facing it, then I am capable of loving it, of looking into it.

Then, is that loneliness of which I am afraid merely a word? Is it not actually a state which is essential, perhaps the door through which I shall find out? That door may lead me further, so that the mind comprehends that state in which it must be alone, uncontaminated. Because all other processes away from that loneliness are deviations, escapes, distractions. If the mind can live with it without condemning it, then perhaps through that the mind will find that state which is alone, a mind that is not lonely but completely alone, not dependent, not seeking to find through something.

It is necessary to be alone, to know that aloneness which is not induced by circumstances, that aloneness which is not isolation, that aloneness which is creativeness, when the mind is no longer seeking either happiness, virtue, or creating resistance. It is the mind which is alone that can find—not the mind which has been contaminated, made corrupt, by its own experiences. So perhaps loneliness, of which we are all aware, if we know how to look at it, may open the door to reality.

Q: I am dependent, primarily psychologically, on others. I want to be free from this dependence. Please show me the way to be free.

K: Psychologically, inwardly, we are dependent, are we not, on rituals, on ideas, people, things, property? We are dependent, and we want to be free from that dependence because it gives us pain. As long as that dependence is satisfactory, as long as I find happiness in it, I do not want to be free. But when the dependence hurts me, when it gives pain, when the thing on which I have depended runs away from me, dies, withers away, looks at somebody else, then I want to be free.

But do I want to be free totally from all psychological dependence, or only from those dependences which give me pain?

Obviously, from those dependences and memories which give me pain. I do not want to be free totally from all dependences, I only want to be free from the particular dependence. So I seek ways and means to free myself, and I ask others, or someone else, to help me to free myself from a particular dependence which causes pain. I do not want to be free from the total process of dependence.

Can another help me to be free from dependence, the partial dependence or the total dependence? Can I show you the way—the way being the explanation, the word, the technique? By my showing you the way, the technique, giving you an explanation, will you be free? You still have the problem, have you not; you still have the pain of it. No amount of my showing you how to deal with it, your discussing it with me, will free you from that dependence. So what is one to do?

Please see the importance of this. You are asking for a method which will free you from a particular dependence or from total dependence. The method is an explanation, is it not, which you are going to practice and live, in order to free yourself? So the method becomes another dependence. In trying to free yourself from a particular dependence, you have introduced another form of dependence.

But if you are concerned with the total freedom from all psychological dependence, if you are really concerned with that, then you will not ask for a method, the way. Then you ask quite a different question, do you not? You ask if you can have the capacity to deal with it, the possibility of dealing with that dependence. So the question is not how to free myself from a dependence, but, 'Can I have the capacity to deal with the whole problem?' If I have the capacity, then I do not depend on anybody. It is only when I say I haven't the capacity that I ask, 'Please help me, show me a way'. But if I have the capacity to deal with a problem of dependence, then I do not ask anyone to help me to dissolve it.

I hope I am making myself clear. I think it is very important not to ask 'How?' but, 'Can I have the capacity to deal with the problem?' Because if I know how to deal with it, then I am free of the problem, so I am no longer asking for a method, the way. Can I have the capacity to deal with the problem of dependence?

Now, psychologically, when you put that question to yourself, what happens? When you consciously put the question, 'Can I have the capacity to free myself from that dependence?' what has happened psychologically? Are you not already free from that dependence? Psychologically, you have depended; and now you say: 'Have I the capacity to free myself?' Obviously, the moment you put that question earnestly to yourself, there is already freedom from that dependence.

I hope you are following not merely verbally, but actually experiencing what we are discussing. That is the art of listening—not merely to listen to my words, but to listen to what is actually taking place in your own mind.

When I know that I can have that capacity, then the problem ceases to be. But because I have not the capacity, I want to be shown. So I create the Master, the guru, the Saviour, someone who is going to save me, who is going to help me. So I become dependent on them. Whereas if I can have that capacity of resolving, understanding the question, then it is very simple, then I am no longer dependent.

This does not mean I am full of self-confidence. The confidence which comes into being through the self, the 'me', does not lead anywhere because that confidence is self-enclosing. But the very question 'Can I have the capacity to discover reality?' gives one an extraordinary insight and strength. The question is not that I have capacity—I have not the capacity—but 'Can I have it?' Then I shall know how to open the door which the mind is everlastingly closing by its own doubts, by its own anxieties, by its fears, experiences, knowledge.

So when the whole process is seen, the capacity is there. But that capacity is not to be found through any particular pattern of action. I cannot comprehend the whole through the particular. Through a particular analysis of a special problem, I shall not comprehend the whole. So can I have the capacity to see the whole—

not to understand one particular incident, one particular happening—but to see the whole total process of my life, with its sorrows, pains, joys, the everlasting search for comfort? If I can put that question in earnestness, then the capacity is there.

With that capacity I can deal with all the problems that arise. There will always be problems, always incidents, reactions; that is life. Because I do not know how to deal with them, I go to others to find out, to ask for the way to deal with them. But when I put the question 'Can I have the capacity?' it is already the beginning of that confidence which is not the confidence of the 'me', of the self, not the confidence which comes into being through accumulation, but that confidence which is renewing itself constantly, not through any particular experience or any incident, but which comes through understanding, through freedom, so that the mind can find that which is real.

Saanen, 26 July 1973

I FEEL IT IS necessary to find out what it means to listen. We are going into something together that requires your attention; not intellectual attention, but the attention to listen, not only to what is being said, but also to listen to what is actually going on within yourself. Listen so as to observe, to actually observe the quality of your mind that is confronting these very complex problems of existence. Not interpreting; then you are not listening. Listening is an action of attention in which there is no interpretation, in which there is no comparison—remembering things which you have read and comparing, or comparing your own experience, to what is being said. Those are all distractions. Actually listen without resistance, without trying to find an answer, because answers do not solve the problem. What does resolve an issue wholly is to be able to observe without the observer, which is the past experience, memory, knowledge—just to observe. With that we can then proceed to find out what sorrow is and whether the human mind can ever be free of it. It is very important to find out for oneself whether sorrow can ever end—actually, not verbally, not intellectually, not romantically, or sentimentally. Because if it ends, then the mind is free of a colossal burden, and that freedom is necessary to inquire into what love is.

So what is sorrow, and is there ever an ending of it? It is really quite a deep problem. I do not know if you have applied your curiosity to it, whether you have seriously undertaken to find out what it is, and whether the mind, your mind—that is, the human mind—can ever go beyond it. We have to find out what pain, grief, and sorrow are. Pain is physiological as well as psychological: suffering, pain in the body, in the organism, and the great complexity of pain and grief and sorrow inwardly, inside the skin as it were, psychologically. All of us know physical pain—a little or a great deal—and we can deal with it medically and in other ways. You can observe pain with a mind that is not attached, with a mind that can observe bodily pain as though from the outside. One can observe one's toothache and not be emotionally, psychologically involved in it. When you are involved emotionally and psychologically with that pain in the tooth, then the pain becomes more, you get terribly anxious, fearful. I do not know if you have noticed this fact.

The key is to be aware of the physical, physiological, biological pain, and in that awareness not get involved with it psychologically. Being aware of the physical pain—and the psychological involvement with it which intensifies the pain and brings about anxiety, fear—and keeping the psychological factor entirely out requires a great deal of awareness, a certain quality of aloofness, a certain quality of unattached observation. Then that pain doesn't distort the activities of the mind; then that physical pain doesn't bring about neurotic activity of the mind. I do not know if you have noticed, when there is a great deal of pain, how the mind, not being able to resolve it, gets involved with the pain and its whole outlook on life is distorted. The awareness of this whole process is not a matter of determination, a matter of a conclusion, or saying that one must be aware; then you create a division and therefore more conflict. Whereas when you intelligently observe the movement of pain and the psychological involvement with that pain, and the distortion in action and in thought, then physical pain can be dealt with, or acted upon, fairly reasonably. That is comparatively easy.

But what is not easy and is rather complex is the whole field of psychological pain, grief, and sorrow. That requires much more, much clearer examination, closer observation and penetration. From childhood we human beings, wherever we are, get hurt.

We have so many scars, consciously or unconsciously; there are so many forms of being hurt. We have shed tears, quietly or openly, and out of that hurt we want to hurt others, which is a form of violence. And being hurt we resist, we build a wall around ourselves never to be hurt again. And when you build a wall around yourself in order not to be hurt, you are going to be hurt much more. From childhood, through comparison, through imitation and conformity, we have stored up these great many hurts and, not being aware of them, all our activity is responses based on these hurts.

Are we going along together? If you are not merely listening to what the speaker is saying, but are using these words to see yourself, then there is a communication between the speaker and yourself.

Can these hurts which produce all kinds of activity, of imbalance, neuroticism, escapes, and so on, be wiped away so that the mind can function efficiently, clearly, sanely, wholly? That is one of the problems of sorrow. You have been hurt, and I am pretty sure that everyone has been. It is part of our culture, it is part of our education. In school you are told you must be as good as 'A', get better marks; you are told that you are not as good as your uncle, or as clever as your grandmother. That is the beginning, and you get more and more brutalized through comparison, not only outwardly, but very, very deeply. And if you don't resolve those hurts, you will go through life wanting to hurt others, or becoming violent, or withdrawing from life, from every relationship, in order never to be hurt again.

As this is a part of our suffering, can the mind that has been hurt become totally free of every form of hurt, and never be hurt again? A mind that is never hurt, and can never be hurt again, is really an innocent mind. That is the meaning of that word in the dictionary—a mind that is incapable of being hurt—and it is therefore incapable of hurting another. Now, how is it possible for a mind that has been hurt deeply, or in passing, to be free of this hurt? How do you answer that question? How do you find out, knowing you are hurt, how to be free of that hurt? If you understand one hurt totally, deeply, completely, then you have understood all the other hurts, for in the one all are included, one hasn't to go chasing one hurt after another. Why is the mind hurt? All forms of education, as it is now, are a process of distorting the mind through competition, through conformity, in the schools and in the family, in all our outward relationships. To be determined not to be hurt is a conclusion of thought, but thought—being time, being a movement, thought which has created the image that it should never be hurt—has not resolved the problem of being hurt. So thought cannot resolve the hurt. Just listen to what the speaker has to say. Imbibe it, drink it and find out. Thought cannot possibly resolve these hurts; and that is the only instrument that we have, that is the only instrument that we have so carefully cultivated, and when that instrument is not brought into action, we feel lost. Right? But when you realize for yourself that thought, the whole machinery of thinking, will not in any way solve this problem of hurt, intelligence is in operation—the intelligence that is not yours or mine, or anyone else's. Analysis will not resolve the hurts. Analysis is a form of paralysis and it cannot resolve the hurts. So what have you? You see very clearly that you are hurt, and that neither thought nor analysis can resolve it. What takes place in the mind that has seen the truth of the process of thought, with all its associations? It is thought that has created the image about yourself and that image has been hurt.

So when the mind realizes the activities of thought with all its images, analysis, movements, cannot resolve hurt, then the mind observes hurt without any movement. And when it observes it totally, in the way we are describing, then you will see every form of hurt is totally gone; because the hurt is the image you have about yourself, and that image has been created by thought. What is hurt is the image, and that image has no reality. It is a verbal structure, a linguistic image, which has been fed by thought, and when the energy of thought is not active, then the image is not. Then there is no possibility of ever being hurt. Got it? Test it. Apply it—not tomorrow, now.

That is one of the causes of our sorrow. And there is the sorrow of loneliness, the sorrow of not having a companion—or if you have a companion, of losing that companion—or the death of someone whom you thought you loved, who gave you physical and psychological satisfaction—both sensory satisfaction and psychological fulfilment. When that person is gone, that is, when that person is dead or turned away from you, all the anxieties, the fears, the jealousies, the loneliness, the despair, the anger, the violence, bursts in you. That is part of our life. Not being able to solve it, in the Asiatic world they say, 'Next life, my friend, we will solve it. After all, there is always the next life, then I will know how to deal with it'. And in the Western world, the sorrow is invested in one person, or one image whom you worship—the suffering of mankind invested in one individual; you also escape through that, but you haven't solved this problem. You have postponed it, you have put it away in an image on a cross in a church. But it is still there.

So sorrow can end only with knowing the movement of yourself: how you want to escape from it; how you want to find an answer to it; and not being able to find an answer, how you resort to beliefs, to images, to concepts. That is what human beings have done throughout the ages; and there are always the priests, the go-betweens who will help you to escape. To observe all this within yourself, which is knowing oneself not according to any psychologist, modern or ancient, but just observing oneself—the hurts, the escapes, the loneliness, the despair, the sense of agony, of never being able to go beyond 'what is'—just to watch that without any movement of thought requires great attention. That attention is, itself, its own discipline, its own order.

Can you observe loneliness, which is one of the factors of our sorrow, or the feeling that you must fulfil in something, and not being able to fulfil, without being frustrated, just watch all that without any movement of thought verbally, or any desire to go beyond it? Let me put it differently. I lose my brother or my son. He dies, and I am paralysed with the shock of it for a few days. Then out of that, at the end of it, I am full of sorrow, pain, loneliness, at the meaninglessness of life; I am left with myself. So remain completely without any movement of thought which says, 'I must go beyond this, I must find my brother, I must communicate with him, I feel lonely, I feel desperate'. Just observe without any movement of thought. Then you will see that out of that suffering comes passion, which has nothing whatsoever to do with lust, which is energy completely free of the movement of thought.

So through—no, I won't use the word *through*—so in that awareness of the whole movement of the 'me', which is the product of thought, which is the movement in time, awareness of the nature and the structure of the 'me', conscious as well as unconscious, there is an ending of sorrow. You can test this for yourself. If you don't test it, you have no right to listen to it, it has no meaning. Through self-knowing there is the ending of sorrow and therefore the beginning of wisdom.

Now, let's go into the next question and consider what love is. I really don't know what it is. One can describe it, one can put it into words, into the most poetic language, using very beautiful words, but words are not love. Sentiment is not love. It has nothing to do with emotions, with patriotism, with ideas; that you know very well, if you go into it. So we can brush aside completely the verbal descriptions, the images that we have built around that word: patriotism, God, work for your country and Queen—you know all that tommy-rot! We also know, if we observe very carefully, that pleasure is not love. Can you swallow that pill? For most of us, love is sexual pleasure. For most of us, this sense of sexual, physical pleasure has become extraordinarily important in the Western world, and now it is pushing towards the Eastern civilizations. When it is denied, there is torture, violence, brutality, extraordinary emotional scenes. Is all that love?

The pleasure of the sexual act and the remembrance of it—chewing the cud over it and wanting it again—the repetition, the pursuit of pleasure, is what is called *love*. We have made that word so vulgar, meaningless: Go and kill for the love of your country; join this group because they love God! We have made that word into a terrible thing, an ugly, vulgar, brutal thing. Life is much bigger, vaster, more deep, than mere pleasure, but this civilization, culture, has made pleasure the most dominant, powerful thing in life. So what is love? What place has it in human relationship between man and woman?

Let us consider what love is in human relationship. When you look at the map of human beings—man, woman, man and woman in relationship with their neighbour, with the state, and all the rest of it—what place has this thing called love in relationship? Has it any place at all in actuality? Life is relationship; life is action in relationship. What place has love in that action?

Are we sharing all this together? Please do; it is your life. Don't waste your life. You have a few years; don't waste them. You are wasting it, and it is a sad thing to see this happen.

So what place has love in relationship? What is relationship, to be related? That means to respond adequately, completely to each other. The meaning of that word *relationship* is to be related; related means in direct contact with another human being, both psychological as well as physiological direct contact. Are we related at all with each other? I may be married, have children, sex, and all the rest of the business, but am I related at all? And what am I related to? I am related to the image that I have built about you or her. Please watch this. Do watch it. And she is related to me according to the image that she has about me. Right? So these two images have relationship; and that imaginary relationship is called love! See how absurd we have made the whole thing. That is a fact. That is not a cynical description. I have built the image about her through the years, or ten days, or a week—or one day is enough. And she has done the same thing. Do you understand the cruelty, the ugliness, the brutality, the viciousness of these images about each other? And the contact of these two images is called relationship. Therefore there is always a battle between the man and the woman, one trying to dominate the other. One having dominated, a culture is built around that domination—the matriarchal system or the patriarchal system. You know what goes on. Is that love?

If it is, then love is merely a word that has no meaning. Because love is not pleasure, jealousy, envy, division between the man and the woman, one dominating the other, one driving the other, possessing the other, being attached to the other. That certainly is not love—it is just a matter of convenience and exploitation. And this we have accepted as the norm of life. When you observe it, really observe it, are totally aware of it, then you will see that you will never build an image—whatever she does or you do there is no image-forming. And perhaps out of that comes an extraordinary flower, the flowering of this thing called love. And it does happen. That love has nothing to do with 'my' or 'your'. It is love. And when you have that, you will never send your children to train in the army, to be killed. Then you will produce quite a different kind of civilization, a different culture, different human beings, man and woman.

Saanen, 23 July 1974

WE HAVE BEEN talking over together the nature and the structure of thought, its place and its limitations, and all the processes and functions involved in the movement of thought. If I may this morning—and it is rather lovely after all these days of rain and cloud to see the mountains, the shadows and the rivers, and the pleasant smell of the air—I would like to talk about responsibility, which is to be answerable. Observing objectively, without any opinion or judgment, we see what is going on in the world: war, appalling misery, and confusion. Who is responsible, or answerable, for all this?

To really find the right response, the right answer, we must look at the whole phenomenon of existence. At the one end you have the extraordinary development of technology, which is almost destroying the earth; at the other end you have what may be called the hope, the demand, the entreating of God, truth, or what you will. There is this vast spectrum, and we seem to answer only to a very small part of it. There is this vast field of existence, of our daily living, and we seem to be incapable of responding to the whole of it. We must find out for ourselves what is the right response, what is the right answer to all this. If we are responsible merely to a very small part of it—ourselves and our little circle, and our little desires, our petty little responsibilities, our selfish, enclosed movement—

neglecting the whole of it, then we are bound to create suffering not only for ourselves, but for the whole of mankind.

❖

IS IT POSSIBLE to be responsible to the whole of mankind? And therefore be responsible to nature, be responsible—that is, to answer adequately, totally—to your children, to your neighbour, to all the movement that man has created in his endeavour to live rightly. To feel that immense responsibility, not only intellectually, verbally, but very deeply, to be able to answer to the whole human struggle, pain, brutality, violence and despair, to respond totally to that, one must know what it means to love. You know that word *love* has been so misused, so spoilt, so trodden upon, but we will have to use that word and give to it a totally different kind of meaning. To be able to answer to the whole, there must be love. To understand that quality, that compassion, that extraordinary sense of energy which is not created by thought, we must understand suffering. When we use the word *understand*, it is not a verbal or intellectual communication of words, but the communication or communion that lies behind the word. Now, first we must understand, and be able to go beyond, suffering. Otherwise we cannot possibly understand the responsibility to the whole, which is real love.

We are partaking, not only verbally, intellectually, but going far beyond that, and to share it is our responsibility. That means you must also hear the word, listen to the semantic meaning of the word, and also share in the movement of self-inquiry, and go beyond it. One must take part in this whole movement; otherwise you will treat it merely verbally or intellectually or emotionally, and then it is nothing.

To understand this responsibility to the whole, and therefore that strange quality of love, one must go beyond suffering. What is suffering? Why do human beings suffer? This has been one of the great problems of life for millions of years. And apparently, very, very, very few have gone beyond suffering, and they either become heroes or saviours, or some kind of neurotic leaders, or religious leaders, and there they remain. But ordinary human beings like you and me and others never seem to go beyond it. We seem to be caught in it. We are asking whether it is possible for you to be really free of suffering.

❖

APPARENTLY, MAN HAS not been able to resolve psychological suffering. He has been able to escape from it, through activities—religious, economic, social, political, business, various forms of escapes like drugs—never confronting the actual fact of suffering. What is suffering? Is it possible for the mind to be completely free of the psychological activity that brings about suffering?

One of the major reasons for suffering is the sense of isolation, the feeling of total loneliness. That is, to feel that you have nothing to depend upon, that you have no relationship with anyone, that you are totally isolated. You have had this feeling, I am quite sure. You may be with your family, in a bus, or at a party, and you have moments of an extraordinary sense of isolation, an extraordinary sense of lack, of total nothingness. That is one of the reasons for suffering. Psychologically, suffering comes through attachment—to an idea, to ideals, to opinions, to beliefs, to persons, to concepts. Please observe it in yourself. The world is the mirror in which you are looking that shows the operations of your own mind. So look there.

Another cause of suffering is a great sense of loss, loss of prestige, loss of power, loss of so many things, and the loss of somebody whom you think you love—and there is death, the ultimate suffering. Now, can the mind be free of all this? Otherwise do what it will, it cannot possibly know this sense of love for the whole. If there is no love for the whole of existence, not only your own but of total humanity, then there is no compassion, then you will never understand what love is. In the love of the whole, the particular comes in. But when there is the particular love, of the one, then there is the absence of the other.

So it is absolutely imperative that we understand and go beyond suffering. Is that possible? Is it possible for the mind to understand this sense of deep inward loneliness, which is different from aloneness? Please don't mix the two. There is a difference between loneliness, and being deeply alone. We will understand what it means to be alone when we understand what the significance of loneliness is. When you feel lonely, it is rather frightening, rather depressing, and you have various kinds of moods from that. Without rationalizing, can you observe it without any movement of escape?

Can I be aware of loneliness without rationalizing, without trying to find the cause of it, just observe, and in that observation discover that escape is through attachment to an idea, to a concept, to a belief. Can I be aware of that belief and how it is an escape? When I observe it quietly, the escape and the belief disappear without any effort. The moment I introduce effort, then there is the observer and the observed, and therefore conflict, but when I am aware of all the implications of loneliness, then there is no observer, there is only the fact of this feeling of being utterly isolated. This isolation takes place also through our daily activity—my ambition, my greed, my envy, concern with my own desire to fulfil, to become somebody, to improve myself. I am so concerned with my beastly little self, and that is part of my loneliness. During the day, during sleep, in all the activities I do, I am so concerned about myself: 'me' and 'you', 'we' and 'they'. I am committed to myself. I want to do things for myself in the name of my nation, in the name of my God, in the name of my family, in the name of my wife.

So this loneliness comes into being through daily activities of self-concern, and when I become aware of all the implications of loneliness, I see all this. I see it, not theorize about it. When I look at something, the details come out. When you look closely at a tree, at a river, or a mountain, or a person, then in that observation you see everything. It tells you, you don't tell it. When you so observe, or when you are so greatly, without any choice, aware of this loneliness, then the thing disappears altogether.

❖

ONE OF THE causes of suffering is attachment. Being attached and finding it is painful, we try to cultivate detachment, which is another horror. Why is the mind attached? An attachment is a form of occupation for the mind. If I am attached to you, I am thinking about you, I am worrying about you. I am concerned about you in my self-centred way because I don't want to lose you, I don't want you to be free, I don't want you to do something which disturbs my attachment. In that attachment I feel somewhat secure. So in attachment there is fear, jealousy, anxiety, suffering. Now, just look at it. Don't say, 'What am I to do?' You can't do anything. If you try to do something about your attachment, then you are trying to create another form of attachment. Right? So just observe it. When you are attached to a person or an idea, you dominate that person, you want to control that person, you deny freedom to that person. When you are attached, you are denying freedom altogether. If I am attached to a Communist ideal, then I bring destruction to others.

If the mind sees that loneliness, attachment, is one of the causes of sorrow, is it possible for the mind to be free of attachment? Which doesn't mean that the mind becomes indifferent, because we are concerned with the whole of existence, not just my existence. Therefore I must respond to, answer to, the whole, and not my particular little desire to be attached to you and wanting to get over that little anxiety of pain and jealousy. Because our concern is to find this quality of love which can only come into being when the mind is concerned with the whole and not with the particular. When it is concerned with the whole, there is love, and then from the whole the particular has a place.

And there is the suffering of loss, of losing somebody whom you 'love'—you understand, I am using that word *love* in quotation marks. Why do you suffer? I lose my son, my mother, my wife. I lose somebody; why do I suffer? Is it that I am suddenly left, hurt very deeply through the death of another? Is it because I have identified myself with that person? It is *my* son, I want him, I am myself projected in that son. I have identified myself with that person, and when that person is no longer there I feel a tremendous sense of hurt because I have nobody to continue me in another. So I am deeply hurt. From that hurt arises self-pity. Please do examine all this. I am not so much concerned about the other; I am really concerned about myself through the other, and therefore I am hurt when the other is not. From that hurt, which is very deep, arises self-pity and the desire to find somebody else through whom I can survive.

There is not only the personal suffering, but the vast suffering of man, the suffering which wars have brought to innocent people, to people who have been killed, to the killer and the killed, the mother, the wife, the children. Whether in the Far East, the Middle East, or in the West, there is this vast human suffering, both physically and psychologically. Unless the mind understands this whole problem, I can play with the word *love*, I can do social work and talk about the love of God, the love of man, the love of all this, but in my heart I will never know what it is. So is my mind, your mind, your consciousness, capable of looking at this fact, looking at it and seeing what extraordinary misery it causes not only to another but to oneself? See how you deprive another of his freedom when you are attached; and when you are attached, you are depriving yourself of your own freedom. And so the battle begins between you and me. Can the mind observe this?

It is only with the ending of suffering that wisdom comes into being. Wisdom is not a thing that you buy in books, or that you learn from another. Wisdom comes in the understanding of suffering and all the implications of suffering, not only the personal, but also the human suffering that man has created. It is only when you go beyond it that wisdom comes into being.

Then to understand, or come upon this thing that we call love, I think we must also understand what beauty is. May I go into it? Beauty. You know it is one of the most difficult things to put into words, but we will try.

Do you know what it means to be sensitive? Not sensitive to your desires, to your ambitions, to your hurts, to your failures, and to your successes—that is fairly easy. Most of us are sensitive to our own little demands, to our own little pursuits of pleasure, fear, anxiety, and delights. But we are talking of being sensitive—not *to* something, but being sensitive—both psychologically and physically. Physically, to be sensitive is to have a very good subtle body—healthy, sane, not overeating, indulging—a sensitive body. That you can try if you are interested. We are not dividing the psyche from the body, it is all interrelated; but you cannot be sensitive psychologically if there is any kind of hurt. Psychologically, we human beings are hurt greatly. We have deep unconscious and conscious wounds, either self-inflicted or caused by others. At school, at home, in the bus, in the office, in the factory, we are hurt. That deep hurt, conscious or unconscious, makes us psychologically insensitive, dull. Watch your own hurt, if you can. A gesture, a word, a look, is enough to hurt. And you are hurt when you are compared with somebody else, when you are trying to imitate somebody else, when you are conforming to the pattern—whether that pattern is set by another or by yourself. So we human beings are deeply wounded; and those wounds bring about neurotic activity—all beliefs are neurotic, ideals are neurotic. Is it possible to understand these hurts and be free of them, never to be hurt again in any circumstances? I am hurt from childhood by various incidents or accidents, a word, a gesture, a look, a slighting, being ignored. There are these wounds. Can they be wiped away without leaving a mark? Watch it please. Don't look somewhere else, look at yourself. You have these wounds. Can they be wiped away not leaving a mark?

If there is a hurt, you are not sensitive, you will never know what beauty is. You can go to all the museums in the world, compare Michelangelo to Picasso, be expert in explanation and in the study of these people and their paintings, their structure and so on, but as long as a human mind is hurt and therefore insensitive, it will never know what beauty is—in the things man has made, in the line of a building, and in the mountain, in the beautiful tree. If there is any kind of inward hurt you will never know what beauty is, and without beauty there is no love. So can your mind know it has been hurt, be aware of those hurts, and not react to those hurts at the conscious or unconscious level?

It is fairly easy to be aware of conscious hurts. Can you know your unconscious hurts; or must you go through all the idiotic process of analysis? I'll go into analysis very quickly and get rid of it. Analysis implies the analyser and the analysed. Who is the analyser? Is he different from the analysed? If he is different, why is he different? Who created the analyser to be different from the analysed? If he is different, how can he know what the thing is? So the analyser *is* the analysed. That is so obvious. To analyse, each analysis must be totally complete. That means if there is any slight misunderstanding, in the next analysis you cannot analyse completely because of previous misunderstandings. Analysis implies time. You can go on endlessly for the rest of your life analysing and you will be still analysing as you are dying.

So how is the mind to uncover the unconscious, deep wounds, the wounds which the race has collected? When the conqueror subjugates the victim, he has hurt him. That is a racial hurt. To the imperialist everybody is beneath him, and he leaves a deep, unconscious hurt on those whom he has conquered. It is there. How is the mind to uncover all these hidden hurts, deep in the recesses of one's consciousness? I see the fallacy of analysis, so there is no analysis. Please watch this carefully. There is no analysis, and our tradition is to analyse, so I have put aside the tradition of analysis. Are you doing this? So what has happened to the mind when it has denied, or put aside, seen the falseness of something, the falseness of analysis? Isn't it free of that burden? Therefore it has become sensitive; it is lighter, clearer, it can observe more sharply. So by putting aside a tradition which man has accepted—analysis, introspection, and so on—the mind has become free. And by denying the tradition, you have denied the content of the unconscious. The unconscious is tradition: tradition of religion, tradition of marriage, tradition of a dozen things. And one of the traditions is to accept hurt and, having accepted hurt, to analyse it to get rid of it. Now, when you deny that because it has been false, you have denied the content of the unconscious. Therefore you are free of the unconscious hurts. You don't have to analyse the unconscious or your dreams.

So by observing hurt and not using the traditional instrument to wipe away that hurt, which is analysis, which is talking it over together—you know all the business that goes on, group therapy and individual therapy and collective therapy—the mind wipes away by being aware, being aware of the tradition. When you deny that tradition, you deny the hurt that accepts that tradition. The mind then becomes extraordinarily sensitive—the mind being the body, the heart, the brain, the nerves. The total thing becomes sensitive.

Now, we are asking what beauty is. We said it is not in the museum, it is not in the picture, it is not in the face, it is not a response to the background of your tradition. When the mind puts all that aside because it is sensitive and because suffering has been understood, you have passion—*there is* passion. Passion is different from lust, obviously. Lust is the continuation of pleasure and the demand for pleasure in different forms. When there is no hurt, when there is the understanding of suffering and going beyond it, then there is that quality of passion which is totally necessary to understand the extraordinary sense of beauty. That beauty cannot possibly exist when the 'me' is constantly asserting. You may be a marvellous painter, accepted by the world as the greatest painter, but if you are concerned with your beastly little self, you are no longer an artist. You are only furthering through art your own selfish continuation.

A mind that is free has gone beyond this sense of suffering; it is free from all hurt and therefore capable of never being hurt again in any circumstances. Whether it is flattered or insulted, nothing can touch it—which doesn't mean it has built a resistance. On the contrary, it is excellently vulnerable. Then you will begin to find out what love is. Obviously, love is not pleasure. Now, we can say that it is not pleasure, not before, because now you have been through all that and put it aside. You can still enjoy the mountains, the trees, and the rivers, the nice faces and the beauty of the land; but when that beauty of the land becomes the pursuit of pleasure, it ceases to be beauty. So love is not pleasure. Love is not the pursuit or the avoidance of fear. Love is not attachment. Love has no suffering. Obviously. And that love means the love of the whole, which is compassion. And that love has its own order, order both within and without; that order cannot be brought about through legislation. Now, when you understand this and live it daily—otherwise it has no value at all, it is just a lot of words without any meaning, just ashes—then life has quite a different significance.

Madras, 5 February 1950

Questioner: We all experience loneliness; we know its sorrow and see its causes, its roots. But what is aloneness? Is it different from loneliness?

Krishnamurti: Loneliness is the pain, the agony of solitude, the state of isolation when you as an entity do not fit in with anything, neither with the group, nor with the country, with your wife, with your children, with your husband; you are cut off from others. You know that state. Now, do you know aloneness? You take it for granted that you are alone; but are you alone?

Aloneness is different from loneliness, but you cannot understand it if you do not understand loneliness. Do you know loneliness? You have surreptitiously watched it, looked at it, not liking it. To know it, you must commune with it with no barrier between it and you, no conclusion, prejudice, or speculation; you must come to it with freedom and not with fear. To understand loneliness, you must approach it without any sense of fear. If you come to loneliness saying that you already know the cause of it, the roots of it, then you cannot understand it. Do you know its roots? You know them by speculating from outside. Do you know the inward content of loneliness? You merely give it a description, and the word is not the thing, the real. To understand it, you must come to it without any sense of getting away from it. The very thought of getting away from loneliness is in itself a form of inward insufficiency. Are not most of our activities an avoidance? When you are alone, you switch on the radio, you do pujas, run after gurus, gossip with others, go to the cinema, attend races, and so on. Your daily life is to get away from yourselves, so the escapes become all-important and you wrangle about the escapes, whether drink, or God. The avoidance is the issue, though you may have different means of escape. You may do enormous harm psychologically by your respectable escapes, and I, sociologically, by my worldly escapes; but to understand loneliness all escapes must come to an end, not through enforcement, compulsion, but by seeing the falseness of escape. Then you are directly confronting 'what is', and the real problem begins.

What is loneliness? To understand it, you must not give it a name. The very naming, the very association of thought with other memories of it, emphasizes loneliness. Experiment with it and see. When you have ceased to escape, you will see that until you realize what loneliness is, anything you do about it is another form of escape. Only by understanding loneliness can you go beyond it.

The problem of aloneness is entirely different. We are never alone; we are always with people except, perhaps, when we go for solitary walks. We are the result of a total process made up of economic, social, climatic, and other environmental influences, and as long as we are influenced, we are not alone. As long as there is the process of accumulation and experience, there can never be aloneness. You can imagine that you are alone by isolating yourself through narrow individual, personal activities, but that is not aloneness. Aloneness can be, only when influence is not. Aloneness is action which is not the result of a reaction, which is not the response to a challenge or a stimulus. Loneliness is a problem of isolation, and we are seeking isolation in all our relationships, which is the very essence of the self, the 'me'—my work, my nature, my duty, my property, my relationship. The very process of thought, which is the result of all the thoughts and influences of man, leads to isolation. To understand loneliness is not a bourgeois act; you cannot understand it as long as there is in you the ache of that undisclosed insufficiency which comes with emptiness, frustration. Aloneness is not an isolation, it is not the opposite of loneliness; it is a state of being when all experience and knowledge are not.

Q: You have talked about relationship based on usage of another for one's own gratification, and you have often hinted at a state called love. What do you mean by love?

K: We know what our relationship is—a mutual gratification and use, though we clothe it by calling it *love*. In usage there is tenderness for and the safeguarding of what is used. We safeguard our frontier, our books, our property; similarly, we are careful in safeguarding our wives, our families, our society, because without them we would be lonely, lost. Without the child the parent feels lonely; you hope that what you are not, the child will be, so the child becomes an instrument of your vanity. We know the relationship of need and usage. We need the postman and he needs us, yet we don't say we love the postman. But we do say that we love our wives and children, even though we use them for our personal gratification and are willing to sacrifice them for the vanity of being called patriotic. We know this process very well, and obviously, it cannot be love. Love that uses, exploits, and then feels sorry cannot be love, because love is not a thing of the mind.

Now, let us experiment and discover what love is—discover, not merely verbally, but by actually experiencing that state. When you use me as a guru and I use you as disciples, there is mutual exploitation. Similarly, when you use your wife and children for your furtherance, there is exploitation. Surely, that is not love. When there is use, there must be possession; possession invariably breeds fear, and with fear come jealousy, envy, suspicion. When there is usage, there cannot be love, for love is not something of the mind. To think about a person is not to love that person. You think about a person only when that person is not present, when he is dead, when he has run off, or when he does not give you what you want. Then your inward insufficiency sets the process of the mind going. When that person is close to you, you do not think of him; to think of him when he is close to you is to be disturbed, so you take him for granted—he is there. Habit is a means of forgetting and being at peace so that you won't be disturbed. So usage must invariably lead to invulnerability, and that is not love.

What is that state when usage—which is thought process as a means to cover the inward insufficiency, positively or negatively—is not? What is that state when there is no sense of gratification? Seeking gratification is the very nature of the mind. Sex is sensation which is created, pictured by the mind, and then the mind acts or does not act. Sensation is a process of thought, which is not love. When the mind is dominant and the thought process is important, there is no love. This process of usage, thinking, imagining, holding, enclosing, rejecting, is all smoke, and when the smoke is not, the flame of love is. Sometimes we do have that flame, rich, full, complete; but the smoke returns because we cannot live long with the flame, which has no sense of nearness, either of the one or the many, either personal or impersonal. Most of us have occasionally known the perfume of love and its vulnerability, but the smoke of usage, habit, jealousy, possession, the contract and the breaking of the contract—all these have become important for us, and therefore the flame of love is not. When the smoke is, the flame is not; but when we understand the truth of usage, the flame is. We use another because we are inwardly poor, insufficient, petty, small, lonely, and we hope that, by using another, we can escape. Similarly, we use God as a means of escape. The love of God is not the love of truth. You cannot love truth; loving truth is only a means of using it to gain something else that you know, and therefore there is always the personal fear that you will lose something that you know.

You will know love when the mind is very still and free from its search for gratification and escapes. First, the mind must come entirely to an end. Mind is the result of thought, and thought is merely a passage, a means to an end. When life is merely a passage to something, how can there be love? Love comes into being when the mind is naturally quiet, not made quiet, when it sees the false as false and the true as true. When the mind is quiet, then whatever happens is the action of love, it is not the action of knowledge. Knowledge is mere experience, and experience is not love. Experience cannot know love. Love comes into being when we understand the total process of ourselves, and the understanding of ourselves is the beginning of wisdom.

Sources and Acknowledgments

From the recording of the public talk at Madras, 16 December 1972, copyright © 1972/1993 Krishnamurti Foundation Trust, Ltd.

From the recording of the public talk at Brockwood Park, 11 September 1971, copyright © 1971/1993 Krishnamurti Foundation Trust, Ltd.

From the report of a talk with students at Rajghat School, Varanasi, 19 December 1952, in volume VII, *The Collected Works of J. Krishnamurti*, copyright © 1991 The Krishnamurti Foundation of America.

From the report of the public talk in Bombay, 12 February 1950, in volume VI, *The Collected Works of J. Krishnamurti*, copyright © 1991 The Krishnamurti Foundation of America.

From the report of the public talk at Ojai, 28 August 1949, in volume V, *The Collected Works of J. Krishnamurti*, copyright © 1991 The Krishnamurti Foundation of America.

From the report of the public talk in Bombay, 12 March 1950, in volume VI, *The Collected Works of J. Krishnamurti*, copyright © 1991 The Krishnamurti Foundation of America.

From the report of the public talk in New York, 18 June 1950, in volume VI, *The Collected Works of J. Krishnamurti*, copyright © 1991 The Krishnamurti Foundation of America.

From the report of the public talk in Seattle, 6 August 1950, in volume VI, *The Collected Works of J. Krishnamurti*, copyright © 1991 The Krishnamurti Foundation of America.

From the report of the public talk at Madras, 3 February 1952, in volume VI, *The Collected Works of J. Krishnamurti*, copyright © 1991 The Krishnamurti Foundation of America.

"Loneliness," from *Commentaries on Living First Series*, copyright © 1956 Krishnamurti Writings, Inc.

From the recording of a discussion with Professor Maurice Wilkins at Brockwood Park, 12 February 1982, copyright © 1982/1993 Krishnamurti Foundation Trust, Ltd.

From *The Awakening of Intelligence*, New York, 24 April 1971, copyright © 1973 Krishnamurti Foundation Trust, Ltd.

From the recording of the public dialogue at Brockwood Park, 30 August 1977, copyright © 1977/1993 Krishnamurti Foundation Trust, Ltd.

From the recording of the public talk at Saanen, 18 July 1978, copyright © 1978/1993 Krishnamurti Foundation Trust, Ltd.

From the recording of the public talk at Bombay, 31 January 1982, copyright © 1982/1993 Krishnamurti Foundation Trust, Ltd.

"With Young People in India," from *Life Ahead*, copyright © 1963 Krishnamurti Writings, Inc.

From *Talks and Dialogues Saanen 1968*, 18 July 1968, copyright © 1970 The Krishnamurti Foundation London.

From the report of the public talk at Saanen, 5 August 1962, in volume XIII, *The Collected Works of J. Krishnamurti*, copyright © 1992 The Krishnamurti Foundation of America.

From the report of the public talk in Bombay, 21 February 1965, in volume XV, *The Collected Works of J. Krishnamurti*, copyright © 1992 The Krishnamurti Foundation of America.

From the report of the public talk in London, 7 April 1953, in volume VII, *The Collected Works of J. Krishnamurti*, copyright © 1991 The Krishnamurti Foundation of America.

From the recording of the public talk at Saanen, 26 July 1973, copyright © 1973/1993 Krishnamurti Foundation Trust, Ltd.

From the recording of the public talk at Saanen, 23 July 1974, copyright © 1974/1993 Krishnamurti Foundation Trust, Ltd.

From the report of the public talk at Madras, 5 February 1950, in volume VI, *The Collected Works of J. Krishnamurti*, copyright © 1991 The Krishnamurti Foundation of America.

Other books by Krishnamurti

On God
On Relationship
On Self-Knowledge
The Revolution from Within
A Wholly Different Way of Living
The Ending of Time
Krishnamurti on Education
Life Ahead
A Timeless Spring: Krishnamurti at Rajghat
Krishnamurti's Notebook
Commentaries on Living First Series
Commentaries on Living Second Series
Commentaries on Living Third Series
Freedom from the Known

Further information about Krishnamurti books and tapes can be obtained from:

Krishnamurti Foundation India
Vasanta Vihar, 64 Greenways Road
Chennai – 600 028.
E-mail: kfihq@md2.vsnl.net.in

Krishnamurti Foundation Trust Ltd.
Brockwood Park, Bramdean,
Hampshire S024 0LQ, England.
E-mail: info@brockwood.org.uk

Krishnamurti Foundation of America
P.O. Box 1560, Ojai,
CA 93024-1560, U.S.A.
E-mail: kfa@kfa.org

Fundacion Krishnamurti Lationamericana
No 59, 1 Ext. Drcha,
28015 Madrid, Spain.
E-mail: **anadonfk@.ddnet.es**